THE CHALLENGE of JESUS

Rediscovering Who Jesus Was and Is

N.T. WRIGHT

InterVarsity Press
Downers Grove, Illinois

InterVarsity Press
P.O. Box 1400, Downers Grove, IL 60515
World Wide Web: www.ivpress.com
E-mail: mail@ivpress.com

InterVarsity Press® is the book-publishing division of InterVarsity Christian Fellowship/USA®, a student movement active on campus at hundreds of universities, colleges and schools of nursing in the United States of America, and a member movement of the International Fellowship of Evangelical Students. For information about local and regional activities, write Public Relations Dept., InterVarsity Christian Fellowship/USA, 6400 Schroeder Rd., P.O. Box 7895, Madison, WI 53707-7895.

All Scripture quotations are the author's translation unless otherwise noted.

Cover illustration: Erich Lessing/Art Resource, N.Y.

ISBN 0-8308-2200-3

Printed in the United States of America ♻

Library of Congress Cataloging-in-Publication Data

Wright, N. T. (Nicholas Thomas)
   The challenge of Jesus : rediscovering who Jesus was & is / N.T. Wright.
     p.   cm.
   Includes bibliographical references.
   ISBN 0-8308-2200-3 (cloth : alk. paper)
   1. Jesus Christ—Historicity. 2. Christian life.   I. Title.
BT303.2.W75   1999
232—dc21

99-36481
CIP

17	16	15	14	13	12	11	10	9	8	7	6	5	4	3
12	11	10	09	08	07	06	05	04	03	02	01	00		

For Simon Kingston
Friend & publisher

CONTENTS

Preface

On January 2, 1999 (my parents' 52nd wedding anniversary, as it happens), Chicago had its worst snowstorm in over thirty years. All day the blizzard raged, shutting major highways and bringing suburban life to a near standstill. For the previous three days I had been able to see the lakeshore from my hotel window only two blocks away; now I could scarcely see the other side of the street.

That evening, as the snowplows struggled around the streets and the airline phones were jammed with callers transferring from canceled flights, I gave my fourth and final address at a remarkable conference. The first of its kind, it brought together under the auspices of the InterVarsity Christian Fellowship over a thousand graduate students and university professors from all across North America, and some from beyond, under the twin title: "Following Christ/Shaping our World." I was privileged to be able to lead some of the thinking with four lectures that now form the backbone of this book. I have tidied them up a little and developed or polished the argument here and there, but they remain quite close to what was said at the time. Several of those present urged me to make the material available in published form, and I am grateful to InterVarsity Press and SPCK for their ready cooperation. It is perhaps important to say that, whereas in my larger scholarly projects I am addressing readers of any and all backgrounds, in the present work I am specifically talking to my fellow-Christians.

The first three lectures, corresponding to chapters two, four and five, presented in brief summary form the historical portrait of Jesus of Nazareth for which I have argued in various places, notably in my book *Jesus and the Victory of God* (London and Minneapolis: SPCK and

Fortress, 1996). That book, to which reference should be made throughout the first five chapters of this book for fuller detail and documentation, stands on the shoulders of its predecessor in the series Christian Origins and the Question of God, namely, *The New Testament and the People of God* (SPCK/Fortress, 1992). I have added, as an introductory chapter, the substance of a lecture I gave at the annual conference of the Anglican Institute, held in Birmingham, Alabama, in April 1997. This lecture in its original form was published in *The Truth About Jesus*, ed. Donald Armstrong (Grand Rapids, Mich.: Eerdmans, 1998), pp. 4-25. I have also added the present chapter three, which attempts to fill in, in more detail, some necessary parts of the picture of Jesus' proclamation of the kingdom of God.

The fourth lecture, corresponding to chapter eight, moves on beyond my previous publications in this area to address various issues in the contemporary church and world, not least the challenges that face Christians in professional and academic life. To prepare for this I have added chapter six on the resurrection, and chapter seven, which applies the story of Easter to the contemporary cultural situation.

I have three concerns throughout the present work. The first is for historical integrity in talking about Jesus. Many Christians have been, frankly, sloppy in their thinking and talking about Jesus, and hence, sadly, in their praying and in their practice of discipleship. We cannot assume that by saying the word *Jesus*, still less the word *Christ*, we are automatically in touch with the real Jesus who walked and talked in first-century Palestine, the Jesus who, according to the letter to the Hebrews, is the same yesterday, today and forever. We are not at liberty to manufacture a different Jesus. Nor will it do to suggest that because we have the Gospels in our New Testaments, we know all we need to about Jesus. As the material presented here will show, and the longer works will reveal in much more detail, Christian traditions have often radically misunderstood the picture of Jesus in those Gospels, and only by hard, historical work can we move toward a fuller comprehension of what the Gospels themselves were trying to say.

The second concern is for the Christian discipleship that professes to follow the true Jesus. The disciplines of prayer and Bible study need to be rooted again and again in Jesus himself if they are not to become idolatrous or self-serving. We have often muted Jesus' stark challenge, remaking him in our own image and then wondering why our personal spiritualities have become less than exciting and life-changing. Throughout what follows I hope to be addressing this, at least implicitly. As one conference participant said to me after the final session, the Jesus whom I describe is an exciting and deeply interesting human being—something that could not always be said for the stained-glass Christ-figure of much Christian imagination, whether in the Catholic, Protestant, Orthodox or evangelical traditions.

Third, I have been particularly concerned to put into the minds, hearts and hands of the next generation of thinking Christians the Jesus-shaped model of, and motivation for, a mission that will transform our world in the power of Jesus' gospel. Those in the universities and professions of our world who desire to be loyal Christians need to think afresh through the issues of what allegiance to Jesus means in practice. It is not enough to say one's prayers in private, maintain high personal morality and then go to work to rebuild the tower of Babel. The substance and structure of the different aspects of our world need to be interrogated in the light of the unique achievement of Jesus and of our commission to be for the world what he was for the Israel of his day.

This last concern explains why, in the final two chapters in particular, I have been at pains to address, albeit briefly, the question of our present cultural climate in the Western world. The loose and sometimes misleading label of *postmodernity* serves as a signpost to many features of our culture that are both disturbing and challenging. Some Christians find this deeply threatening. I believe that the message of

Jesus Christ enables us to look these issues in the face, recognizing the ways in which postmodernity has a point to make that we dare not ignore but insisting that we must now go through it and out the other side into new tasks and possibilities. Just as integrity demands that we think clearly and rigorously about Jesus himself, so it also demands that we think clearly and rigorously about the world in which we follow him today, the world we are called to shape with the loving, transforming message of the gospel.

N. T. Wright
May 1999

CHAPTER ONE

THE CHALLENGE
OF STUDYING JESUS

A FRIEND OF MINE, LECTURING IN A THEOLOGICAL COLLEGE IN KENYA, introduced his students to "The Quest for the Historical Jesus." This, he said, was a movement of thought and scholarship that in its earlier forms was carried on largely in Germany in the eighteenth and nineteenth centuries. He had not gone far into his lecture explaining this search for Jesus when one of his students interrupted him. "Teacher," he said ("I knew I was in trouble," my friend commented, "as soon as he called me 'teacher'!"), "if the Germans have lost Jesus, that is their problem. We have not lost him. We know him. We love him."

Research into Jesus himself has long been controversial, not least among devout Christians. Several people in the wider Christian world wonder if there is anything new to say about Jesus and if the attempt to say something fresh is not a denial either of the church's traditional teaching or of the sufficiency of Scripture. I want to grasp this nettle right away and explain why I regard it, not just as permissible but as vitally necessary that we grapple afresh with the question of who Jesus was and therefore who he is. In doing so I in no way want to deny or undermine the knowledge of Jesus of which the Kenyan student spoke and which is the common experience of the church down the centuries and across widely differing cultures. I see the historical task, rather, as part of the appropriate activity of knowledge and love, to get to know even better the one whom we claim to know and follow. If even in a human relationship of knowledge and love there can be misunderstandings, false impressions, wrong assumptions, which need to be teased out and dealt with, how much more when the one to whom we are relating is Jesus himself.

I believe, in fact, that the historical quest for Jesus is a necessary and nonnegotiable aspect of Christian discipleship and that we in our generation have a chance to be renewed in discipleship and mission precisely by means of this quest. I want to explain and justify these beliefs from the outset. There are, however, huge problems and even dangers within the quest, as one would expect from anything that is heavy with potential for the kingdom of God, and I shall need to say something about these as well.

There are well-known pitfalls in even addressing the subject, and we may as well be clear about them. It is desperately easy when among like-minded friends to become complacent. We hear of wild new theories about Jesus. Every month or two some publisher comes up with a blockbuster saying that he was a New Age guru, an Egyptian freemason or a hippie revolutionary. Every year or two some scholar or group of scholars comes up with a new book full of imposing footnotes to tell us that Jesus was a peasant Cynic, a wandering wordsmith or the preacher of liberal values born out of due time.

The day I was redrafting this chapter for publication, a newspaper article appeared about a new controversy, initiated by animal-rights activists, as to whether Jesus was a vegetarian.

We may well react to all this sort of thing by saying that it is all a waste of time, that we know all we need to know about Jesus, and there is no more to be said. Many devout Christians taking this line content themselves with an effortless superiority: we know the truth, these silly liberals have got it all wrong, and we have nothing new to learn. Sometimes people like me are wheeled out to demonstrate, supposedly, the truth of "traditional Christianity," with the implied corollary that we can now stop asking these unpleasant historical questions and get on with something else, perhaps something more profitable, instead.

Some, however, react by reaching for equally misleading alternative stereotypes. A defense of a would-be "supernatural" Jesus can easily degenerate into a portrayal of Jesus as a first-century version of Superman—not realizing that the Superman myth is itself ultimately a dualistic corruption of the Christian story. There are several Jesus-pictures on offer that appear very devout but that ignore what the New Testament actually says about the human being Jesus of Nazareth or what it meant in its original context.

I do not intend to encourage any of these attitudes. I repeat: I regard the continuing historical quest for Jesus as a necessary part of ongoing Christian discipleship. I doubt very much if in the present age we shall ever get to the point where we know all there is to know and understand all there is to understand about Jesus, who he was, what he said and what he did, and what he meant by it all. But since orthodox Christianity has always held firm to the basic belief that it is by looking at Jesus himself that we discover who God is, it seems to me indisputable that we should expect always to be continuing in the quest for Jesus precisely as part of, indeed perhaps as the sharp edge of, our exploration into God himself.

This, of course, carries certain corollaries. If it is true that Christian faith cannot preempt the historical questions about Jesus, it is also true that historical study cannot be carried out in a vacuum. We have been taught by the Enlightenment to suppose that history and faith are antithetical, so that to appeal to the one is to appeal away from the other. As a result, historians have regularly been suspect in the community of faith, just as believers have always been suspect in the community of secular historiography. When Christianity is truest to itself, however, it denies precisely this dichotomy—uncomfortable though this may be for those of us who try to live in and to speak from and to both communities simultaneously. Actually, I believe this discomfort is itself one aspect of a contemporary Christian vocation: as our world goes through the deep pain of the death throes of the Enlightenment, the Christian is not called to stand apart from this pain but to share it. I shall say more about this in the concluding chapter. I am neither a secular historian who happens to believe in Jesus nor a Christian who happens to indulge a fancy for history. Rather, I am someone who believes that being a Christian necessarily entails doing business with history and that history done for all it's worth will challenge spurious versions of Christianity, including many that think of themselves as orthodox, while sustaining and regenerating a deep and true orthodoxy, surprising and challenging though this will always remain.[1]

Let me then move to the positive side. What are the reasons that make it imperative for us to study Jesus?

The Necessity of the Quest

The most basic reason for grappling with the historical question of Jesus is that we are made for God: for God's glory, to worship God and reflect his likeness. That is our heart's deepest desire, the source of our deepest vocation. But Christianity has always said, with John 1:18, that nobody has ever seen God but that Jesus has revealed God. We shall only discover who the true and living God actually is if we take the risk of looking at Jesus himself. That is why the contemporary debates about Jesus are so important; they are also debates about God himself.

The second reason why I engage in serious historical study of Jesus is out of loyalty to Scripture. This may seem deeply ironic to some on both sides of the old liberal-conservative divide. Many Jesus scholars of the last two centuries have of course thrown Scripture out of the window and reconstructed a Jesus quite different from what we find in the New Testament. But the proper answer to that approach is not simply to reassert that because we believe in the Bible we do not need to ask fresh questions about Jesus. As with God so with the Bible; just because our tradition tells us that the Bible says and means one thing or another, that does not excuse us from the challenging task of studying it afresh in the light of the best knowledge we have about its world and context, to see whether these things are indeed so. For me the dynamic of a commitment to Scripture is not "we believe the Bible, so there is nothing more to be learned," but rather "we believe the Bible, so we had better discover all the things in it to which our traditions, including our 'protestant' or 'evangelical' traditions, which have supposed themselves to be 'biblical' but are sometimes demonstrably not, have made us blind." And this process of rethinking will include the hard and often threatening question of whether some things that our traditions have taken as "literal" should be seen as "metaphorical," and perhaps also vice versa—and, if so, which ones.

This leads to the third reason, which is the Christian imperative to truth. Christians must not be afraid of truth. Of course, that is what many reductionists have said, as with apparent boldness they have whittled down the meaning of the gospel to a few bland platitudes, leaving the sharp and craggy message of Jesus far behind. That is not my agenda. My agenda is to go deeper into the meaning than we have before and to come back to a restatement of the gospel that grounds the things we have believed about Jesus, about the cross, about the resurrection, about the incarnation, more deeply within their original setting. When I say the great Christian creeds—as I do day-by-day in worship—I mean them from the heart, but I find that after twenty years of historical study I mean something much deeper, much more challenging, than I meant when I started. I cannot compel my readers to follow me in this particular pilgrimage, but I can and do hold out an invitation to see Jesus, the Gospels, ourselves, the world and, above all, God in what may well be a new and perhaps disturbing light.

The fourth reason for undertaking the study of Jesus is because of the Christian commitment to mission. The mission of most Christians likely to read this book takes place in a world where Jesus has been a hot topic for several years now. In America particularly, Jesus—and the quest for him—has been featured in *Time* magazine, on television and elsewhere in the media. And the people whom ordinary Christians meet, to whom they must address the gospel, have been told over and over by the media, on the basis of some recent book or other, that the Jesus of the Gospels is historically incredible and that Christianity is therefore based on a mistake. It simply will not do to declare this question out-of-bounds, to say that the church's teaching will do for us, thank you very much, so we do not need to ask historical questions. You cannot say that to a serious and enquiring person who engages you in conversation on a train or to someone who wanders into a church one Sunday and asks what it is all about. If Christianity is not rooted in things that actually happened in first-century Palestine, we might as well be Buddhists, Marxists or almost anything else. And if Jesus never existed, or if he was quite different from what the Gospels and the church's worship affirms him to have been, then we are indeed living in cloud-cuckoo-land. The skeptics can and must be answered, and when we do so we will not merely reaffirm the traditions of the church, whether Protestant, Catholic, evangelical or whatever. We will be driven to reinterpret them, discovering depths of meaning within them that we had never imagined.

One of the reasons why we had not imagined some of the depths that, I believe, are actually there to be found lies in our own historical and cultural setting. I am a first-century historian, not a Reformation or eighteenth-century specialist. Nevertheless, from what little I know of the last five hundred years of European and American history, I believe that we can categorize the challenge of the eighteenth-century Enlightenment to historic Christianity in terms of its *asking a necessary question in a misleading fashion.* The divide in contemporary Christianity between liberals and conservatives has tended to be between those who, because they saw the necessity of asking the historical question, assumed that it had to be asked in the Enlightenment's fashion and those on the other hand who, because they saw the misleadingness of the Enlightenment's way of asking the question, assumed that the historical question was itself unnecessary. Let me speak first of the necessity of the Enlightenment's question and then of the misleading way it has been addressed.

To understand why the Enlightenment's historical question was necessary we need to take a further step back to the Protestant Reformation of the sixteenth century. The protest of the Reformation against the medieval church was not least a protest in favor of a *historical* and *eschatological* reading of Christianity against a timeless system. Getting at the literal *historical* meaning of the texts, as the Reformers insisted we must, meant historical reading: the question of what Jesus or Paul really meant, as opposed to what the much-later church said they meant, became dramatically important. Go back to the beginning, they said, and you will discover that the developed system of Roman Catholicism is based on a mistake. This supported the Reformers' *eschatological* emphasis: the cross was God's once-for-all achievement, never to be repeated, as the Reformers saw their Catholic opponents doing in the Mass. But, arguably, the Reformers never allowed this basic insight to drive them beyond a halfway house when it came to Jesus himself. The Gospels were still treated as the repositories of true doctrine and ethics. Insofar as they were history, they were the history of the moment when the timeless truth of God was grounded in space and time, when the action that accomplished the timeless atonement just happened to take place. This, I know, is a gross oversimplification, but I believe it is borne out by the sequel. Post-Reformation theology grasped the insights of the reformers as a new set of timeless truths and used them to set up new systems of dogma, ethics and church order in which, once again, vested interests were served and fresh thought was stifled.

The Enlightenment was, among many other things, a protest against a system that, since it was itself based on a protest, could not see that it was itself in need of further reform. (The extent to which the Enlightenment was a secularized version of the Reformation is a fascinating question, one for brave Ph.D. candidates to undertake rather than the subject for a book like this. But we have to do business at least with these possibilities if we are to grasp where we have come from and hence where we may be being called to go to.) In particular, the Enlightenment, in the person of Hermann Samuel Reimarus (1694-1768), challenged unthinking would-be Christian dogma about the eternal son of God and his establishment of the oppressive system called "Christianity." Reimarus challenged it in the name of history—the same weapon that the reformers had used against Roman Catholicism. Go back to the beginning, he said, and you will discover that Christianity is based on a mistake. Jesus was, after all, another in a long line of failed Jewish revolutionaries. Christianity as we know it was the invention of the early disciples.[2]

I believe that Reimarus's question was necessary. *Necessary* to shake European Christianity out of its dogmatism and to face a new challenge—to grow in understanding of who Jesus actually was and what he actually accomplished. *Necessary* to challenge bland dogma with a living reality; *necessary* to challenge idolatrous distortions of who Jesus actually was and hence who God actually was and is, with a fresh grasp of truth. The fact that Reimarus gave his own question an answer that is historically unsustainable does not mean he did not ask the right questions. Who was Jesus, and what did he accomplish?

This necessity has been underlined in our own century, as Ernst

Käsemann saw all too clearly. Look what happens, he said in a famous lecture in 1953, when the church abandons the quest for Jesus. The nonquesting years between the wars created a vacuum in which nonhistorical Jesuses were offered, legitimating the Nazi ideology. I would go so far as to suggest that whenever the church forgets its call to engage in the task of understanding more and more fully who Jesus actually was, idolatry and ideology lie close at hand. To renounce the quest because you do not like what the historians have so far come up with is not a solution.

But the Enlightenment's raising of the question of Jesus was done in a radically misleading manner, which still has profound effects on the research of today. The Enlightenment notoriously insisted on splitting apart history and faith, facts and values, religion and politics, nature and supernature, in a way whose consequences are written into the history of the last two hundred years—one of the consequences being, indeed, that each of those categories now carries with it in the minds of millions of people around the world an implicit opposition to its twin, so that we are left with the great difficulty of even conceiving of a world in which they belong to one another as part of a single indivisible whole. Again, so much debate between *liberals* and *conservatives* has taken place down this fault line (history *or* faith, religion *or* politics and so on), while the real battle—the challenge to rearticulate a reintegrated worldview—has not even been attempted. But there is a deeper problem with the Enlightenment than its radically split worldview. The real problem is that it offered a rival *eschatology* to the Christian one. This needs a little explanation.

Christianity, as we shall see, began with the thoroughly Jewish belief that world history was focused on a single geographical place and a single moment in time. The Jews assumed that their country and their capital city was the place in question, and that the time, though they did not know quite when it would be, would be soon. The living God would defeat evil once and for all and create a new world of peace and justice. The early Christians believed that this had in principle happened in and through Jesus of Nazareth; as we shall see, they believed this (a) because Jesus himself had believed it and (b) because he had been vindicated by God after his execution. This is what early Christian eschatology was all about: not the expectation of the literal end of the space-time universe but the sense that world history was reaching, or indeed had reached, its single intended climax.

This, as we saw, was grasped in principle by the Reformers. Martin Luther, it is true, used the captivity and exile of Israel in Babylon as a controlling metaphor for his understanding of church history, in which the church, like Israel, had been suffering a "Babylonian captivity" for many centuries until his own day. But his strong focus on Jesus himself prevented this from becoming a new rival eschatology, divorced from its first-century roots. Even though Luther saw his own day as a special time in which God was doing a new thing, this remained for him strictly derivative: the real new day had dawned, once and for all, with Jesus himself. His own new "great light" did not upstage the Light of the World himself.

With the Enlightenment, however, this further step was taken. All that had gone before was a form of captivity, of darkness; now, at last, light and freedom had dawned. World history was finally brought to its climax, its real new beginning, not in Jerusalem but in Western Europe and America, not in the first century but in the eighteenth. (We may perhaps be allowed a wry smile at the way in which post-Enlightenment thinkers to this day heap scorn upon the apparently ridiculous idea that world history reached its climax in Jerusalem two thousand years ago, while themselves holding a view we already know to be at least equally ridiculous.) Thus, as long as the necessary question of the Enlightenment (the question of the historical Jesus) was addressed within the Enlightenment's own terms, it was inevitable not only that christology would collapse into warring camps of naturalist and supernaturalist—in other words, that Jesus-pictures would be produced in which the central character was either an unexceptional first-century Jew or an inhuman and improbable superman-figure—but also that liberal and conservative alike would find it hugely difficult to reconceive the first-century Jewish eschatological world within which alone the truly historical Jesus belongs. Jesus was almost bound to appear as the teacher of either liberal timeless truths or conservative timeless truths. The thought that he might have been the turning point of history was, to many on both sides of the divide, almost literally unthinkable. Even Albert Schweitzer, who brought the eschatological perspective back with a bang to the study of Jesus, radically misunderstood it.

Schweitzer did, however, alert Christian thinkers to something that has taken almost a century to assimilate: that the world in which Jesus lived, and which he addressed with his message about the kingdom, was a world in which the Jewish expectation of God's climactic and decisive action within history was uppermost. It is this, I believe, that has given fresh impetus to the study of Jesus and makes it imperative that we engage in this study. Properly conceived, Schweitzer's answer to Reimarus's question—that Jesus belongs within the world of this first-century Jewish expectation—enables us to see that by engaging in the study of Jesus himself we can understand much better—better indeed than the Reformers—what it meant within Jesus' own world that God would act in a one-off, unique way, generating a response that would not be a repetition of that initial act but rather the appropriation and implementation of it.

I believe, then, that within the multiple tasks to which God is calling the church in our own generation, there remains the necessary task of addressing the Enlightenment's question as to who precisely Jesus was and what precisely he accomplished. And I believe that there are ways of addressing this question that do not fall into the trap of merely rearranging the Enlightenment's own categories. We have a new opportunity in our generation to move forward in our thinking, our praying, our whole Christian living, no doubt by many means, but not least by addressing the question of the historical Jesus in fresh and creative ways.

All of this drives me to explore the human, historical, cultural and political setting and meaning of what the Gospels say about Jesus. This ought not to be seen by orthodox Christians as a threat. Granted, the contemporary orthodox Christian tradition to which I and many of my readers have fallen heir was conceived and stated against a background of modernist and secularist reductionism. In that setting it was vital to affirm, as orthodox Christians have regularly done in the last two centuries or so, the God-givenness of Scripture, the divinity of Jesus and so on. But our earlier forebears in the faith were well-aware that there were errors in the opposite direction as well—patterns of belief and behavior that saw Jesus as a demigod, not really human at all, striding through the world as a divine, heroic figure, untroubled by human questions, never wrestling with vocation, aware of himself as someone from outside the whole system, telling people how they might escape the wicked world and live forever in a different realm altogether. This is the worldview out of which there grew—and still grows—gnosticism, that many-sided system of thought and spirituality in which a secret knowledge (*gnosis*) can be attained that will enable humans to rediscover their lost secret identity and thereby, escaping the present world, enjoy bliss in an entirely different sphere of reality.

Gnosticism in one or other of its many forms has been making a huge comeback in our day. Sometimes this has been explicit, as for instance in the New Age movements and similar spiritualities that encourage people to discover who they *really* are. Just as often, though, gnosticism of a different sort has been on offer within would-be mainstream traditional orthodoxy, as many Christians have embraced a Jesus who only *seemed* to be human, have read a Bible that only *seemed* to have human authors, have looked for a salvation in which God's created order became quite irrelevant, a salvation thought of in almost entirely dualist fashion. Woe betide us if, in our commitment to winning yesterday's battles against reductionist versions of Christianity, we fail to engage in tomorrow's, which might be quite different.

New Opportunities in the Quest

But why then should we suppose that there is anything new to say about Jesus? This is a question I am often asked, not least by journalists on the one hand and by puzzled, nonacademically inclined Christians on the other. The answer, actually, is that there both is and is not. Mere novelty is almost bound to be wrong: if you try to say that Jesus did not announce the kingdom of God or that he was in fact a twentieth-century thinker born out of due time, you will rightly be rejected. But what did Jesus mean by the kingdom of God? That and a thousand other cognate questions are far harder than often supposed, and the place to go to find new light is the history of Jesus' own time. And that means first-century Judaism, in all its complexity and with all the ambiguities of our attempts to reconstruct it.

There are, of course, all sorts of new tools available to help us to do this. We have the Dead Sea Scrolls, all of them at last in the public domain. We have good new editions of dozens of hitherto hard-to-find Jewish texts, and a burgeoning secondary literature about them. We have all kinds of archaeological finds, however complex they may be to interpret. Of course, there is always the danger both of oversimplification and overcomplication. Our sources do not enable us to draw a complete sociological map of Galilee and Judaea in Jesus' day. But we know enough to be able to say quite a lot, for instance, about the agenda of the Pharisees; quite a lot, too, about what sort of aspirations came to be enshrined in what we call apocalyptic literature and why; quite a lot, too, about Roman agendas in Palestine and the agendas of the chief priests and the Herodian dynasty in their insecure struggles for a compromised power. Quite a lot, in other words, about the necessary contexts for understanding Jesus.

We can perhaps say something, too, about Galilean peasants. Not, I think, everything that some current writers would like us to. There are those who see the peasant culture of ancient Mediterranean society as the dominant influence in the Galilee of Jesus' day, with the Jewish apocalyptic coloring decidedly muted; so that Jesus' announcement of the kingdom has less to do with specifically Jewish aspirations and more to do with the kind of social protest that might arise in any culture.[3] Let me stress *both* that this is a mistake *and* that showing it to be so does not lessen the element of social protest that is still to be found within the much wider-ranging and more theologically grounded kingdom-announcement that we can properly attribute to Jesus. Equally, I emphasize that one of the things we can know about peasant societies like that of Jesus is that they were heavily dependent upon oral traditions, not least traditions of instant storytelling. When we get this right, we avoid at a stroke some of the extraordinary reductionism that has characterized the so-called Jesus Seminar, with its attempt to rule out the authenticity of most Jesus-stories on the grounds that people would only have remembered isolated sayings, not complete stories.[4] But my overall point is simply this: there is a great deal of history writing still waiting to be attempted and accomplished, and we have more tools to do it with than most of us can keep up with. If we really believe in any sense in the incarnation of the Word, we are bound to take seriously the flesh that the Word became. And since that flesh was first-century Jewish flesh, we should rejoice in any and every advance in our understanding of first-century Judaism and seek to apply those insights to our reading of the Gospels.

And we do so, we must insist, not in order to undermine what the Gospels are saying or to replace their stories with quite different ones of our own, but to understand what it is that they are really all about.

It is a standard objection to historical-Jesus research to say that God has given us the Gospels and that we cannot and should not put a construction of our own in their place. But this misunderstands the nature of the task. Precisely because these texts have been read and preached as holy Scripture for two thousand years, all kinds of misunderstandings have crept in, which have then been enshrined in church tradition. The historian will often see not necessarily that the Gospels need to be rejected or replaced but that they did not in fact mean what subsequent Christian tradition thought.

Let me take an obvious example that will be of further interest as our topic proceeds. Martin Luther rightly reacted against the medieval translation of *metanoeite* as *paenitentiam agere* ("do penance") and insisted that the word referred originally to the "repentance" that takes place deep within the human heart, not in the outward actions prescribed as a quasi-punishment. He could not know that his reading would be used, in turn, to support an individualistic and pietistic reading of Jesus' command to repent, which does no justice at all to the meaning of the word in the first century. Jesus was summoning his hearers to give up their whole way of life, their national and social agendas, and to trust him for a different agenda, a different set of goals. This of course included a change of heart, but went far beyond it.[5]

This illustrates a point that could be repeated dozens of times. Historical research, as I have tried to show in various places, by no means tells us to throw away the Gospels and substitute a quite different story of our own. It does, however, warn us that our familiar readings of those Gospel stories may well have to submit to serious challenges and questionings and that we may end up reading even our favorite texts in ways we had never imagined. Since this agenda is thus truly Protestant, truly Catholic, truly evangelical and truly liberal, not to mention potentially charismatic as well, those in all kinds of streams within the church should be able to embrace it as their own. It takes a certain courage, of course, to be prepared to read familiar texts in new ways. It is abundantly worth it. What you lose in terms of your regular readings will be more than made up for in what you will gain.

False Trails in the Quest

In order to understand where we are in the bewildering options in today's quest, it helps to see the state of play a hundred years ago.[6] Three figures stand out. William Wrede argued for consistent skepticism: we cannot know very much about Jesus, he certainly did not think of himself as the Messiah or the Son of God, and the Gospels are basically theological fiction. Albert Schweitzer argued for consistent eschatology: Jesus shared the first-century apocalyptic expectation of the end of all things, and though he died without it having come about, he started the eschatological movement that became Christianity. What is more, the Synoptic Gospels more or less got him right. Over against both these positions Martin Kähler argued that the quest for a purely historical Jesus was based on a mistake since the real figure at the heart of Christianity was the preached and believed Christ of the church's faith, not some figment of the historian's imagination.

All three positions are alive and well as we come to the end of the twentieth century. The Jesus Seminar and several writers of a similar stamp stand in the line of Wrede. Sanders, Meyer, Harvey and several others, myself included, stand in the line of Schweitzer. Luke Timothy Johnson is our contemporary Kähler, calling down a plague on all the houses.[7] Since I have been criticized, sometimes quite sharply, for offering this sort of analysis of the current state of play, I want to say a word or two of explanation and perhaps even justification.

Schweitzer's construction of Jesus, as is well-known, was so unwelcome to the theological establishment that there followed half a century of little serious Jesus-research. The so-called New Quest of the

1950s and 1960s made some progress at getting things started again but never really managed to recover a serious historical nerve. Books and articles spent more time arguing about criteria for authenticity than offering major hypotheses about Jesus himself. By the mid-1970s there was a sense of stalemate. It was then that quite a new style of Jesus historiography began to emerge, explicitly distinguishing itself from the so-called New Quest. For my money, the best book of that period was Ben Meyer's *The Aims of Jesus,*[8] which received less notice than it should have precisely because it broke the normal mold—and perhaps because it made quite heavy demands on a New Testament scholarly world unused to thinking through its own presuppositions and methods with high philosophical rigor. Six years after Meyer, E. P. Sanders's *Jesus and Judaism*[9] continued the trend. Both books rejected the New Quest's methods; both offered reconstructions of Jesus that made thorough and sustained use of Jewish apocalyptic eschatology; both offered fully blown hypotheses that made a fair amount of sense within first-century Judaism, rather than the bits-and-pieces recon-struction based on a small collection of supposedly authentic but isolated sayings, characteristic of the New Quest.

In this light I suggested in the early 1980s that we were witnessing what I called a "third quest" for Jesus. Despite the way the phrase has sometimes been used since, it was not intended as a blanket term for all 1980s and 1990s Jesus research. It was a way of distinguishing between the new wave I have just described and the continuing New Quest. The events of the last twenty years have, I believe, amply confirmed my judgment. What Meyer, Sanders and several others were doing was significantly different, in several ways that can be laid out unambiguously and reasonably noncontroversially, from the Old Quest of the pre-Schweitzer days and from the New Quest started by Ernst Käsemann and chronicled notably by James M. Robinson.[10] In this light when the Jesus Seminar, then J. Dominic Crossan and then particularly Robert Funk himself, the founder and chair of the Jesus

Seminar, explicitly continued the work of the New Quest, in Funk's case making quite a point of doing so,[11] I believe that I am justified in continuing to distinguish these movements in this way. Of course, contemporary history refuses to stand still and be cut up into neat pieces. Several writers cross over the boundaries this way and that. But I persist both in maintaining the distinction between the Wrede route and the Schweitzer route and in arguing that the latter offers the best hope for serious historical reconstruction.

I have argued in detail against the Jesus Seminar and Crossan in particular in various places, and it would be tedious to repeat such arguments here. But I want to make it clear that if I disagree with Crossan, Funk and the Jesus Seminar, and in different ways with Marcus Borg, as I do, it is not because I think they are wrong to raise the questions they do but because I believe their presuppositions, methods, arguments and conclusions can be successfully controverted on good historical grounds, not by appealing to theological a prioris. It is not enough, nor would it be true, to dismiss such writers as a bunch of disaffected liberals or unbelievers. We must engage in actual arguments about actual issues.

One of the best arguments, however, is the offering of an alternative hypothesis that actually does the job that a successful hypothesis must: make sense of the data, do so with an essential simplicity, and shed light on other areas.[12] It is to that task that we shall presently turn. But let me conclude this chapter with an appeal for others not just to read as interested outsiders about this task, but actually to engage in it themselves.

I have argued that the historical quest for Jesus is necessary for the health of the church. I grieve that in the church both in England and in America there seem to be so few—among a church that is otherwise so well-educated in so many spheres, with more educational resources and helps than ever before—who are prepared to give the time and attention to these questions that they deserve. I long for the day when seminarians will again take delight in the detailed and fascinated study of the first century. If that century was not the moment when history reached its great climax, the church is simply wasting its time.

This is not a task simply for a few backroom specialists. If church leaders themselves spent more time studying and teaching Jesus and the Gospels, a good many of the other things we worry about in day-to-day church life would be seen in their proper light. It has far too often been assumed that church leaders stand above the nitty-gritty of biblical and theological study; they have done all that, we implicitly suppose, before they come to office, and now they simply have to work out the "implications." They then find themselves spending countless hours at their desks running the church as a business, raising money or working at dozens of other tasks, rather than poring over their foundation documents and enquiring ever more closely about the Jesus whom they are supposed to be following and teaching others to follow. I believe, to the contrary, that each generation has to wrestle afresh with the *question* of Jesus, not least its biblical roots if it is to be truly the church at all—not that we should engage in abstract dogmatics to the detriment of our engagement with the world, but that we should discover more and more of who Jesus was and is, precisely in order to be equipped to engage with the world that he came to save. And this is a task for the whole church, especially those appointed to leadership and teaching roles within it.

All our historical study, then, must be done to energize the church in its mission to the world. This is not to say that we are not open to following the argument wherever it goes or that we are not open to reading all texts, both canonical and noncanonical, which may help us in following the historical trail. On the contrary. It is because we believe we are called to be the people of God for the world that we must take the full historical task with utter seriousness. Study all the evidence; think through all the arguments. I am proud to be part of one particular ecclesial tradition, that of the Anglican or Episcopalian church, that has a long and noble history of doing just that (though in recent years this tradition has often been somewhat muted). It has been part of that tradition at its best that it is prepared to think things through afresh—something that other traditions, not least those that think of themselves as "Protestant" or "evangelical," would do well to emulate.

But as we do this, we must remind ourselves again and again—as the liturgies of the traditional churches do in so many ways—that when we are telling the story of Jesus, we are doing so as part of the community that is called to model this story to the world. The more I take part in the quest for Jesus, the more I am challenged by it both as an individual and as a churchman. This is not because what I find undermines traditional orthodoxy, but precisely because the rich, full-blooded orthodoxy I find bubbling up from the pages of history poses challenges to me personally and to all the congregations I know. These challenges are extremely demanding, precisely because they are gospel challenges, kingdom challenges. At this point, being a Quester is simply the same thing as being a disciple. It means taking up the cross and following wherever Jesus leads. And the good and the bad news is that only when we do that will we show that we have truly understood the history. Only when we do that will people take our arguments, whether historical or theological, seriously. Only when we do that will we be the means whereby the Quest, which started so ambiguously as part of the Enlightenment program, can perform the strange purpose that I believe, under God, it came into being to accomplish. Do not be afraid of the Quest. It may be part of the means whereby the church in our own day will be granted a new vision, not just of Jesus, but of God.

So to our topic. As part of our overall quest to follow Jesus Christ and to shape our world according to God's will, we address a set of questions. They can be drawn together into five in particular, which we will examine in what follows:

1. Where does Jesus belong within the Jewish world of his day?

2. What, in particular, was his preaching of the kingdom all about? What was he aiming to do?

3. Why did Jesus die? In particular, what was his own intention in going to Jerusalem that last fateful time?

4. Why did the early church begin, and why did it take the shape it did? Specifically, of course, what happened at Easter?

5. How does all this relate to the Christian task and vision today? How, in other words, does this historical and also deeply theological approach put fire into our hearts and power into our hands as we go about shaping our world?

It is difficult to address all these issues simultaneously. There is a sense in which the reader will only understand the significance of all the parts when the whole is in view. If human maturity is evidenced by delayed gratification, one sign of Christian maturity may be a readiness to hear the argument through to the end, not short-circuiting it in the interests of a quick-fix spirituality or missiology. Patience is as much a virtue in history and theology as it is anywhere else.

CHAPTER TWO

THE CHALLENGE OF THE KINGDOM

W*HAT DID JESUS MEAN WHEN HE SAID THE KINGDOM OF GOD WAS* at hand? Or to put it another way, what did the average Galilean villager hear when a young prophet strode into town and announced that Israel's God was now at last becoming King? The great majority of scholars down the years have agreed that the kingdom of God was central to Jesus' message; but there has been no agreement on what precisely that phrase and the cognate ideas that go with it actually meant. In this chapter, therefore, we must first outline the central core of meaning that the phrase would have for a first-century Jew and then explore Jesus' announcement from three different angles.

Inside First-Century Judaism

To answer our question we have to make a journey as difficult for us in the contemporary Western world as that undertaken by the Wise Men as they went to Bethlehem. We have to think our way back into someone else's world, specifically, the world of the Old Testament as it was perceived and lived by first-century Jews. That is the world Jesus addressed, the world whose concerns he made his own. Until we know how Jesus' contemporaries were thinking, it will not just be difficult to understand what he meant by "the kingdom of God"; it will be totally impossible, as generations of well-meaning but misguided Christian readers have, alas, demonstrated.

At once I sense that some may say, with a measure of reluctance, "All right, I suppose we have to get into that first-century Jewish material; but the only point will be so that once we've seen how Jesus addressed his own culture we can learn to address ours in the same way." There is a tiny grain of truth in that but a much larger lump of misunderstanding. The most important truth lies much, much deeper. Before we can get to the application to our own day, we have to allow fully for the uniqueness of Jesus' situation and position. Jesus, after all, was not just an example of somebody getting it right. Jesus believed and acted upon two vital points, without which we will not even begin to understand what he was all about. These two points are foundational to everything I shall say from now on.

First, he believed that the creator God had purposed from the beginning to address and deal with the problems within his creation *through Israel*. Israel was not just to be an "example" of a nation under God; Israel was to be the means through which the world would be saved. Second, Jesus believed, as did many though not all of his contemporaries, that this vocation would be accomplished through Israel's history reaching a great moment of climax, in which Israel herself would be saved from her enemies and through which the creator God, the covenant God, would at last bring his love and justice, his mercy and truth, to bear upon the whole world, bringing renewal and healing to all creation. In technical language what I am talking about is *election* and *eschatology:* God's choice of Israel to be the means of saving the world; God's bringing of Israel's history to its moment of climax, through which justice and mercy would embrace not only Israel but the whole world.

Put these two beliefs into the first-century context and see what happens. The Jews of Jesus' day, as is well-known, were living under foreign rule and had been for several centuries. The worst thing about that was not the high taxation, the alien laws, the brutality of oppression and so on, awful though that often was. The worst thing was that the foreigners were pagans. If Israel was truly God's people, why were the pagans ruling over her? If Israel was called to be God's true humanity, surely these foreign nations were like the animals over which Adam and Eve were to rule. Why then were they turning into monsters and threatening to trample on God's defenseless chosen people? This state of affairs had existed ever since the Babylonians had come and destroyed Jerusalem in 597 B.C., carrying away the Judaeans captive into exile. Thus, though some of them had returned from *geographical* exile, most believed that the *theological* state of exile was still continuing. They were living within a centuries-old drama, still waiting for the turn in the story that would bring them out on top at last.[1]

Nor were local politics any better. Zealous Jews had long regarded their own local rulers as compromisers, and the Jewish leaders of Jesus' day fell exactly into that category. The powerful Chief Priests were wealthy pseudo-aristocrats who worked the system and got what they could out of it. Herod Antipas (the Herod of the main body of the Gospels, as opposed to his father Herod the Great) was a puppet tyrant bent on wealth and self-aggrandizement. And the popular frustration with the overall rule of Rome and the local rule of the priests and Herod brought together what we must never separate if we are to be true to the biblical witness: religion and politics, questions of God and of the ordering of society. When they longed for the kingdom of God, they were not thinking about how to secure themselves a place in heaven after they died. The phrase "kingdom of heaven," which we find frequently in Matthew's Gospel where the others have "kingdom of God," does not refer to a place, called "heaven," where God's people will go after death. It refers to the rule of heaven, that is, of God, being brought to bear in the present world. Thy kingdom come, said Jesus, thy will be done, *on earth as in heaven.* Jesus' contemporaries knew that the creator God intended to bring justice and peace to his world here and now. The question was, how, when and through whom?

With a certain oversimplification we can trace easily enough the three options open to Jews in Jesus' day. If you go down the Jordan valley from Jericho to Masada, you can see evidence of all of them. First, the quietist and ultimately dualist option, taken by the writers of the Dead Sea Scrolls at Qumran: separate yourself from the wicked world and wait for God to do whatever God is going to do. Second, the compromise option taken by Herod: build yourself fortresses and palaces, get along with your political bosses as well as you can, do as well out of it as you can and hope that God will validate it somehow. Third, the zealot option, that of the Sicarii who took over Herod's old palace/fortress of Masada during the Roman-Jewish war: say your prayers, sharpen your swords, make yourselves holy to fight a holy war, and God will give you a military victory that will also be the theological victory of good over evil, of God over the hordes of darkness, of the Son of Man over the monsters.

Only when we put Jesus into this context do we realize how striking, how dramatic, was his own vocation and agenda. He was neither a quietist nor a compromiser nor a zealot. Out of his deep awareness, in loving faith and prayer, of the one he called "Abba, Father," he went back to Israel's Scriptures and found there another kingdom-model, equally Jewish if not more so. And it is that model we are now to explore. The kingdom of God, he said, is at hand. In other words, God was now unveiling his age-old plan, bringing his sovereignty to bear on Israel and the world as he had always intended, bringing justice and mercy to Israel and the world. And he was doing so, apparently, through Jesus. What could this mean?

God's Plan Unveiled

Throughout his brief public career Jesus spoke and acted as if God's plan of salvation and justice for Israel and the world was being unveiled through his own presence, his own work, his own fate. This idea of the plan being unveiled is, again, characteristically Jewish, and Jesus' contemporaries had developed a complex way of talking about it. They used imagery, often lurid and spectacular, drawn from the Scriptures, to talk about things that were happening in the public world, the world of politics and society, and to give those happenings their theological meaning.

Thus, instead of saying "Babylon is going to fall, and this will be like a cosmic collapse," Isaiah said, "The sun will be darkened, the moon will not give its light, and the stars will be falling from heaven."[2] The Jewish Bible is full of such language, which is often called "apocalyptic," and we would be quite wrong to imagine that it was all meant to be taken literally. It was a way, to repeat the point, of *describing* what we would call space-time events and *investing* them with their theological or cosmic *significance*. Jews of Jesus' day did not, by and large, expect that the space-time universe was going to come to a stop. They did expect that God was going to act so dramatically within the space-time universe, as he had before at key moments like the Exodus, that the only appropriate language would be the language of a world taken apart and reborn.[3]

Jesus inherited this tradition and made it his own in one way in particular. He told stories whose many dimensions cracked open the worldview of his hearers and forced them to come to terms with God's reality breaking in to their midst, doing what they had always longed for but doing it in ways that were so startling as to be hardly recognizable. The parables are Jesus' own commentary on a crisis—the crisis faced by Israel, and more specifically, the crisis brought about by Jesus' own presence and work.

Jesus was not primarily a "teacher" in the sense that we usually give that word. Jesus *did* things and then commented on them, explained them, challenged people to figure out what they meant. He acted practically and symbolically, not least through his remarkable works of healing—works that today all but the most extreme skeptics are forced to regard as in principle historical. In particular, he acted and spoke in such a way that people quickly came to regard him as a prophet. Though, as we shall see, Jesus saw himself as much more than a prophet, that was the role he adopted in his early public career, following on as he did from the prophetic work of John the Baptist. He intended to be perceived, and was indeed perceived, as a prophet announcing the kingdom of God.

But, like many of Israel's prophets of old, in doing this he confronted other kingdom-dreams and kingdom-visions. If his way of bringing the kingdom was the right way, then Herod's way was not, the Qumran way was not and the Zealot way was not. And the Pharisees, who in Jesus' day were mostly inclined toward the Zealot end of the spectrum, were bound to regard him as a dangerous compromiser.[4] We shall see the results of this in the next chapter. Let me, then, unfold briefly the main thrusts of Jesus' kingdom-message under three headings: the end of exile, the call of a renewed people, and the warning of disaster and vindication to come.

The End of Exile

Jesus embarked on a public career of kingdom-initiation. His movement began with John's baptism, which must have been interpreted as a coded dramatization of the exodus, hinting strongly that the new exodus, the return from exile, was about to take place. But Jesus soon became better known for healing than for baptizing. And it was his remarkable healings, almost certainly, that won him a hearing. He was not a teacher who also healed; he was a prophet of the kingdom, first enacting and then explaining that kingdom. I take the healings as read, then, and move on at once to the explanations.

Jesus' parables were not simply shrewd stories about human life and motivation. Nor were they simply childish illustrations, earthly stories with heavenly meanings. Again and again they are rooted in the Jewish Scriptures, in the Jewish narratives that were told and retold officially and unofficially. We could look at these at great length, but there is only space here to glance at two of the best known and to suggest dimensions to them that may be unfamiliar.

I begin with the parable of the sower in Mark 4:1-20 and its parallels.[5] This parable is not simply a wry comment on the way in which many hear the gospel message and fail to respond to it appropriately. Nor is it merely a homely illustration taken from the farming practices of Galilee. It is a typically Jewish story about the way in which the kingdom of God was coming. It has two roots in particular, which help to explain what Jesus was about.

First, it is rooted in the prophetic language of return from exile. Jeremiah and other prophets spoke of God's *sowing* his people again in their own land. The Psalms, at the very point where they are both celebrating the return from exile and praying for it to be completed, sang of those who sowed in tears reaping with shouts of joy. But above all the book of Isaiah used the image of sowing and reaping as a controlling metaphor for the great work of new creation that God would accomplish after the exile. "The grass withers, the flower fades, but the word of our God will stand for ever." "As the rain and snow water the earth, so shall my word be. It shall not return to me empty, but it will accomplish my purpose." New plants, new shrubs, will spring up before you as you return from exile.[6] All this goes back to the story of Isaiah's call in chapter 6, where the prophet sees Israel like a tree being cut down in judgment, and then the stump being burnt; but the holy seed is the stump, and from that stump there shall come forth new shoots.[7]

It is that last passage—Isaiah 6:9-10—that Jesus quotes in Matthew 13:14-15, Mark 4:12 and Luke 8:10 by way of explanation of the parable of the Sower.[8] The parable is about what God was doing in Jesus' own ministry. God was not simply reinforcing Israel as she stood. He was not underwriting her national ambitions, her ethnic pride. He was doing what the prophets always warned: he was judging Israel for her idolatry and was simultaneously calling into being a new people, a renewed Israel, a returned-from-exile people of God.

The second Old Testament root of the parable of the sower is the tradition of apocalyptic storytelling we find in, for instance, the book of Daniel. In Daniel 2, Nebuchadnezzar dreams of a great statue composed of four different metals, with gold at the top and a mixture of iron and clay at the bottom. The statue is demolished, the feet of clay being crushed by a stone, cut out of a mountain, which in turn becomes a mountain that fills the whole earth. So too, in Daniel 7 the four beasts make war on the human figure, one like a son of man, until God takes his seat and the son of man is exalted over the beasts. Even so, says Jesus, the story of God's people is being encapsulated, recapitulated, in his own work. Some seed falls on the path; some on the rock; some among thorns. But some seed falls on good soil and bears fruit, thirtyfold, sixtyfold, a hundred-fold. The kingdom of God, the return from exile, the great climax of Israel's history, is here, Jesus is saying, though it does not look like you thought it would. The parable itself is a parable about parables and their effect: this is the only way that the spectacular truth can be told, and it is bound to have the effect that some will look and look and never see, while others find the mystery sud-denly unveiled, and they see what God is doing.

The second parable that opens a dramatic window on the kingdom of God is the one we call the Prodigal Son, in Luke 15.[9] Among the dozens of things people regularly and often rightly say about this parable, one thing is missed by virtually everybody, though I submit that it would be blindingly obvious to most first-century Jewish listeners. A story about a scoundrel young son who goes off into a far pagan country and is then astonishingly welcomed back home is—of course!—the story of exile and restoration. It was the story Jesus' contemporaries wanted to hear. And Jesus told the story to make the point that *the return from exile was happening in and through his own work.* The parable was not a general illustration of the timeless truth of God's forgiveness for the sinner, though of course it can be translated into that. It was a sharp-edged, context-specific message about what was happening in Jesus' ministry. More specifically, it was about what was happening through Jesus' welcome of outcasts, his eating with sinners.

This story, too, has a dark side to it. The older brother in the story represents those who are opposed to the return from exile as it is actually happening: in this case, the Pharisees and lawyers who see what Jesus is doing and think it scandalous. Jesus' claim is that in and through his own ministry the long-awaited return is actually happening, even though it does not look like what people imagined. The return is happening under the noses of the self-appointed guardians of Israel's ancestral traditions, and they remain blind to it because it doesn't conform to their expectations.

In these two parables and in dozens of other ways Jesus was announcing, cryptically, that the long-awaited moment had arrived. This was the good news, the *euangelion.* We should not be surprised that Jesus in announcing it kept on the move, going from village to village and, so far as we can tell, staying away from Sepphoris and Tiberias, the two largest cities in Galilee. He was not so much like a wandering preacher preaching sermons, or a wandering philosopher offering maxims, as like a politician gathering support for a new and highly risky movement. That is why he chose to explain his actions in the quotation from Isaiah: some must look and look and never see, otherwise the secret police will be alerted. Again, we should not imagine that politics here could be split off from theology. Jesus was doing what he was doing in the belief that in this way Israel's God was indeed becoming king.

Throughout this work Jesus was seeking to gather support for his kingdom-movement. He was calling out a renewed people. This is the second aspect of the kingdom-announcement that we must study.

The Call of the Renewed People

When Jesus announced the kingdom, the stories he told functioned like dramatic plays in search of actors. His hearers were invited to audition for parts in the kingdom. They had been eager for God's drama to be staged and were waiting to find out what they would have to do when he did so. Now they were to discover. They were to become kingdom-people themselves. Jesus, following John the Baptist, was calling into being what he believed would be the true, renewed people of God.

Jesus' opening challenge as reported in the Gospels was that people should "repent and believe." This is a classic example, which I mentioned in the previous chapter, of a phrase whose meaning has changed over the years. If I were to go out on the street in my local town and proclaim that people should "repent and believe," what they would hear would be a summons to give up their private sins (one suspects that in our culture sexual misbehavior and alcohol or drug abuse would come quickly to mind) and to "get religion" in some shape or form—either experiencing a new inner sense of God's presence, or believing a new body of dogma, or joining the church or some sub-branch of it. But that is by no means exactly what the phrase "repent and believe" meant in first-century Galilee.

How are we to unlearn our meanings for such a phrase and to hear it through first-century ears? It helps if we can find another author using it at around the same place and time as Jesus. Consider, for example, the Jewish aristocrat and historian Josephus, who was born a few years after Jesus' crucifixion and who was sent in A.D. 66 as a young army commander to sort out some rebel movements in Galilee. His task, as he describes it in his autobiography,[10] was to persuade the hot-headed Galileans to stop their mad rush into revolt against Rome and to trust him and the other Jerusalem aristocrats to work out a better *modus vivendi*. So when he confronted the rebel leader, he says that he told him to give up his own agenda and to trust him, Josephus, instead. And the word he uses are remarkably familiar to readers of the Gospels: he told the brigand leader to "repent and believe in me," *metanoēsein kai pistos emoi genesesthai*.

This does not, of course, mean that Josephus was challenging the brigand leader (who, confusingly, was called "Jesus") to give up sinning and have a religious conversion experience. It has a far more specific and indeed political meaning. I suggest that when we examine Jesus of Nazareth forty years earlier going around Galilee telling people to repent and believe in him or in the gospel, we dare not screen out these meanings. Even if we end up suggesting that Jesus meant more than Josephus did—that there were indeed religious and theological dimensions to his invitation—we cannot suppose that he meant less. He was telling his hearers to give up their agendas and to trust him for his way of being Israel, his way of bringing the kingdom, his kingdom-agenda. In particular, he was urging them, as Josephus had, to abandon their crazy dreams of nationalist revolution. But whereas Josephus was opposed to armed revolution because he was an aristocrat with a nest to feather, Jesus was opposed to it because he saw it as, paradoxically, a way of being deeply disloyal to Israel's God and to his purpose for Israel to be the light of the world. And whereas Josephus was offering as a counter-agenda a way that they must have seen as compromise, a shaky political solution cobbled together with sticky tape, Jesus was offering as a counter-agenda an utterly risky way of being Israel, the way of turning the other cheek and going the second mile, the way of losing your life to gain it. This was the kingdom-invitation he was issuing. This was the play for which he was holding auditions.

Along with this radical invitation went a radical welcome. Wherever Jesus went, there seemed to be a celebration; the tradition of festive meals at which Jesus welcomed all and sundry is one of the most securely established features of almost all recent scholarly portraits. And the reason why some of Jesus' contemporaries found this so offensive is not far to seek (though not always understood). It was not just that he as an individual was associating with disreputable people; that would not have been a great offense. It was because he was doing so *as a prophet of the kingdom* and was indeed making these meals and their free-for-all welcome a central feature of his program. The meals spoke powerfully about Jesus' vision of the kingdom; what they said was subversive of other kingdom-agendas. Jesus' welcome symbolized God's radical acceptance and forgiveness; whereas his contemporaries would have seen forgiveness and a God-given new start in terms of the Temple and its cult, Jesus was offering it on his own authority and without requiring any official interaction with Jerusalem. (The exception proves the rule: when Jesus healed a leper and told him to go to the priest and make the required offering, the point was of course that an ex-leper needed the official bill of health in order to be readmitted to his community.)[11]

Those who heeded Jesus' call to audition for the kingdom-play that God was staging through him found themselves facing a challenge. Christians from quite early in the church's life have allowed themselves to see this challenge as a new rule book, as though his intention was simply to offer a new code of morality. This has then become problematic within the Reformation tradition in particular, where people have been sensitive about the danger of putting one's human "good works" logically prior to the faith by which one is justified. But that was not the point. Jesus' contemporaries already had a standard of morality to rival any and to outstrip most. They never supposed—and nor did Jesus—that their behavior was what commended them to God; for them—and for Jesus—behavior was what ought to follow from God's initiative and covenant. Such anxious theological discussions miss the real issue. The key thing was that the inbreaking kingdom Jesus was announcing created a new world, a new context, and he was challenging his hearers to become the new people that this new context demanded, the citizens of this new world. He was offering a challenge to his contemporaries to a way of life, a way of forgiveness and prayer, a way of jubilee, which they could practice in their own villages, right where they were.

This is the context, I suggest, within which we should understand what we call the Sermon on the Mount (Mt 5—7), though we do not have the space to look at it in detail here. The Sermon (whether or not it was delivered all at once by Jesus, it certainly represents substantially the challenge he offered to his contemporaries) is not, first and foremost, a private message for individuals to find salvation in Jesus, though of course it includes that in its wider reaches. Nor is it simply a great moral code (though it does of course contain some shining examples of great moral precepts). It makes the sense it does because it depends, all through, on Jesus' kingdom-announcement and on the fact that Jesus himself was, through this announcement, summoning people to follow him in the new way of life, the kingdom-way.

The Sermon is a challenge, in particular, to find a way of being Israel other than the normal revolutionary way. "Do not resist evil"; "turn the other cheek"; "go the second mile"; these are not invitations to be a doormat for Jesus but constitute a warning not to get involved in the ever-present resistance movement. Instead, Jesus' hearers are to discover the true vocation of Israel—to be the light of the world, the salt of the earth. The city set on a hill that cannot be hidden is obviously Jerusalem, designed to be the place where the one true God will reveal himself for all humankind. But at the heart of Jerusalem is the Temple, the house built on the rock. The sermon ends with a coded but very sharp warning. The real new Temple, the real house-on-the-rock, will consist of the community that builds its life upon Jesus' words. All other attempts to create a new Israel, a new Temple (remember that

Herod's Temple was still being completed in Jesus' lifetime), a pure or revolutionary community, would be like building a house on the sand. When the wind and storms came, it would fall with a great crash. Jesus was calling his hearers to take part in God's new drama, the great play in which Israel would at last fulfill her ancient vocation to be the light of the world. This was to be the way of true love and justice through which Israel's God would be revealed to the watching world.

Many of Jesus' hearers could not follow him on his travels, but there were several whom he summoned to do just that. As well as the close circle of the twelve—itself, of course, a deeply symbolic number, clearly indicating Jesus' intention to reconstitute Israel around himself—there were many to whom he issued a challenge to give up all and come with him. Some he commissioned to share in the work of announcing the kingdom, including the actions, the healings and the table-fellowship, which as we shall see later, turned the announcement into symbolic praxis. To take up the cross and follow Jesus meant embracing Jesus' utterly risky vocation—to be the light of the world in a way the revolutionaries had never dreamed of. It was a call to follow Jesus into political danger and likely death, in the faith that by this means Israel's God would bring Israel through her present tribulations and out into the new day that would dawn.

If, therefore, Jesus was embodying and announcing and summoning others to join in with the reconstitution of the people of God and their new direction at the great turning-point of history, the world of thought within which he lived indicated that he would also have expected that this would result in a great turnaround in the history and life of the non-Jewish nations as well. When Israel's God finally does for Israel that which he has promised, then, in much Jewish thought, the effects will ripple out to reach the whole world. The coming King, in many Old Testament texts (e.g., Is 42), would bring God's justice not merely to Israel but to the whole world. Many, said Jesus, will come from east and west and sit down with the patriarchs in the kingdom of God. Jesus does not appear to have said much else on this subject. (This is in itself an interesting sign that, despite much current scholarship, the writers of the Gospels did not feel free to invent all kinds of new sayings to suit their own setting and place them on Jesus' lips; the church was heavily involved in the mission to the Gentiles and its attendant problems, but we would hardly guess this from the Gospels.) He seems to have been conscious of a vocation to focus his own work quite sharply on Israel; once his decisive work was done, then the kingdom-invitation would go out much wider, but the time was not yet.[12]

What, then, did Jesus think was going to happen? How would his kingdom-announcement reach its decisive and climactic moment?

Disaster and Vindication

I have argued thus far that Jesus' kingdom-announcement consisted of his telling and reenacting the story his contemporaries were longing to hear but giving it a radical new twist. The kingdom was coming, was coming indeed in and through his own ministry; but it was not going to look like what they had expected. In the final section of this chapter I want to highlight the conclusion of the story as Jesus was telling it.

He and his contemporaries were living within a controlling story, a great scriptural narrative through which the puzzles of their own times could be discerned (though how this should be done and what might be the results of doing so were of course fiercely contested). The controlling story was often told in terms of the new exodus: when the Egypts of the day, not least their Pharaohs, vaunted themselves against God's people, God would deliver Israel by mighty acts within history and bring his people through their great trials to vindication at last. Sometimes this story was told in apocalyptic terms: the Syrian crisis of the early second century B.C. precipitated one such retelling, with the megalomaniac dictator Antiochus Epiphanes portraying

Pharaoh and (at least in some tellings) the Maccabean resistance fighters playing the gallant Israelites carving out a way for the slaves to be freed. The Syrians were the monsters; the Jews were the human beings, threatened, embattled, but to be vindicated. It was not difficult for Jesus' contemporaries to reapply such stories and such imagery to their own day. The stories that formerly featured Egypt, Babylon and Syria now focused on Rome.

Jesus stood firmly against the retelling of the story that had become customary in his day. God's purpose would not after all be to vindicate Israel as a nation against the pagan hordes, winning the theological battle by military force. On the contrary, Jesus announced, increasingly clearly, that God's judgment would fall not on the surrounding nations but on the Israel that had failed to be the light of the world. Who then would be vindicated in the great coming debacle? Back comes the answer with increasing force and clarity: Jesus himself and his followers. They were now the true, reconstituted Israel. They would suffer and suffer horribly, but God would vindicate them.

A good deal of the material in the Synoptic Gospels is taken up with warnings about a great coming judgment. Christians from very early times have applied this material to the question of what happens both to human beings after their death and to the world as a whole at the great final judgment that is still awaited at the end of history. When we read such passages in their first-century context, however, a rather different picture emerges. The warnings that Jesus issued were, like those of the great prophets before him, warnings of coming judgments of YHWH *within history*; like Jeremiah he prophesied the fall of Jerusalem itself. Jeremiah saw Babylon as the agent of God in punishing his wayward people; Jesus seems to have cast Rome in the same role. And the judgment would come, not as an arbitrary "punishment" by God for Israel's failure to obey some general moral standards but as the inevitable result (not that its inevitability meant that God was not involved in it) of Israel's choosing the way of violence, the way of resistance, rather than following in the way Jesus himself had grasped and articulated in his own life and message. If they would not follow the way of peace, they would reap the consequences.

Some obvious examples: In Luke 13 Jesus' followers tell him about some Galileans whom Pilate had had killed in the sanctuary itself. Jesus' response is interesting: Do you suppose those Galileans were worse sinners than all the others? No, but unless you repent, you will all likewise perish. Or what about the eighteen on whom the tower in Siloam fell and killed? Were they worse sinners than all the others in the Jerusalem area? No, but unless you repent, you will all likewise perish. This is not a warning about frying in hell after death. This is the warning that if Israel refuses to repent of her present flight into national rebellion against Rome, Roman swords in the Temple and falling masonry throughout Jerusalem will become the means of judgment.

The warnings reach their height as Jesus rides into Jerusalem on a donkey and bursts into tears (Lk 19:41-44). "If only you had known, even now," he sobbed, "the things that make for peace; but now they are hidden from your eyes! For the days will come when your enemies will raise up a bank against you, and hem you in on every side, and dash you into pieces, you and your little ones, and leave not one stone upon another, because you did not know the day of your visitation." Once again, this was not a warning about the judgment that faced individuals after their death, nor even, in the first instance, the judgment that, in most Christian tradition, awaits the whole world at the very end. It was the solemn and tragic warning about the fate that Jerusalem was courting for itself by refusing the way of peace that Jesus had held out. These warnings became very specific. Jesus seems to have regarded himself as the last prophet in the great sequence; part of his message was precisely that there would not be another chance. The generation that refused to heed him would be the generation upon whom the judgment would fall.

These warnings cluster together within the so-called Little Apocalypse of Mark 13 and its parallels in Matthew 24 and Luke 21. The whole chapter is to be read, I suggest, as a prediction not of the end of the world but of the fall of Jerusalem. The critical thing, here and elsewhere, is to understand how apocalyptic language works. As I said before, the language of the sun and the moon being darkened, and so forth, is regularly used in Scripture to *denote* major political or social upheavals—the rise and fall of empires, as we say—and to *connote* by the use of this language the cosmic or theological significance that they ascribe to these events.

The language in Mark 13, then, about the Son of Man coming on the clouds should not be taken with wooden literalism—as, of course, generations both of critical scholars and uncritical believers have taken it. The language here is taken from Daniel 7, where the events referred to are the defeat and collapse of the great empires that have opposed the people of God and the vindication of the true people of God, the saints of the most high. The phrase about "the son of man coming on the clouds" would not be read, by a first-century Jew poring over Daniel, as referring to a human being "coming" downwards toward the earth riding on an actual cloud. It would be seen as predicting great events in and through which God would be vindicating his true people after their suffering. They would "come," not to earth but to God.

Jesus was thereby using some standard themes within second-Temple Jewish expectation in a radically new way. He was taking material about the destruction of Babylon, or Syria, or whomever, and was applying it to Jerusalem. And he was redirecting on to himself and his followers the prophetic predictions of vindication.

It is sometimes suggested that views of this sort are in some way anti-Jewish. This misses the whole point. One of the noblest and most deep-rooted traditions in Judaism is that of *critique from within*. The Pharisees were deeply critical of most of their Jewish contemporaries.

The Essenes regarded all Jews except themselves as heading for judgment; they had transferred to themselves all the promises of vindication and salvation, while they heaped anathemas on everyone else, not least the Pharisees. That did not make the Pharisees, or the Essenes, anti-Jewish. The other side of the coin of Jesus' free and open welcome to all and sundry was the warning that those who did not follow in the way he was leading were, by that very refusal, indicating their commitment to the way of being Jewish that involved confrontation with pagan Rome and so pulling down on their own heads the great historical devastation that would result. But the fall of Jerusalem, when it came, would indicate clearly enough that Jesus' way had been right. This would not be the only vindication for Jesus and his kingdom-announcement, but it was a central and essential part of his message. It was a characteristic, if radical, position for a first-century Jew to take.

Conclusion

We may now sum up what we have seen so far about Jesus' announcement of the kingdom. He told the story of the kingdom in such a way as to indicate that Israel's long exile was finally coming to its close. But this was not simply to be good news for all Jews, no matter what their own attitudes to his agenda might be. His retelling of the story was deeply subversive, with sharp polemic reserved for alternative tellings of Israel's story. Jesus was claiming to be speaking for Israel's true ancestral traditions, denouncing what he saw as deviation and corruption at the very heart of Israel's present life.

This picture, I believe, makes very good sense historically. It locates Jesus thoroughly credibly within the world of first-century Judaism. His critique of his contemporaries was a critique from within; his summons was not to abandon Judaism and try something else but to become the true, returned-from-exile people of the one true God. His aim was to be the means of God's reconstitution of Israel. He would challenge and deal with the evil that had infected Israel herself. He would be the means of Israel's God returning to Zion. He was, in short, announcing the kingdom of God—not the simple revolutionary message of the hard-liners but the doubly revolutionary message of a kingdom that would overturn all other agendas, including the revolutionary one. As we shall see in chapter four, he was thereby claiming both the role of Messiah and the vocation of redemptive suffering. As we shall see in chapter five, he was claiming that this was the vocation of Israel's God himself.

It may seem a huge step from the historical Jesus of the first century to our own vocation and tasks, whether professional, practical, academic or whatever. Let me conclude the present chapter by pointing forward to the two ways, about which I shall say more in the final two chapters, through which Christians today might make all this their own.

First, all that we are and do as Christians is based upon the one-off unique achievement of Jesus. It is because he inaugurated the kingdom that we can live the kingdom. It is because he brought the story of God and Israel, and hence of God and the cosmos, to its designed climax that we can now implement that work today. And we will best develop that Christian vocation if we understand the foundation upon which we are building. If we are to follow Jesus Christ we need to know more about the Jesus Christ we are following.

Second, the foundation serves as the model for the building as a whole. What Jesus was to Israel, the church must now be for the world. Everything we discover about what Jesus did and said within the Judaism of his day must be thought through in terms of what it would look like for the church to do and be this for the world. If we are to shape our world, and perhaps even to implement the redemption of our world, this is how it is to be done.

CHAPTER THREE

THE CHALLENGE OF THE SYMBOLS

I HAVE ARGUED SO FAR THAT JESUS IS TO BE LOCATED WITHIN THE Judaism of his day in terms of his activity as a prophet announcing the kingdom of God. More specifically, I have argued that he understood by this the real return from exile, which was taking place in and through his own work, and that he saw this in turn in a doubly revolutionary sense, setting himself not only against Rome and the Herodians, and by implication against the Temple regime, but also against the normal revolutionaries. All of this, I have suggested, we can see in the stories Jesus told, both the fully fledged stories, that is, the parables, and the implicit story within which his kingdom-announcement, even in its briefest forms, belongs, and to which it offered the decisive climax. In this chapter I want to fill in this picture from a different angle, that of symbolic action.

With symbols goes controversy. Tease someone about their nationality if you wish, provided you know them well and they are tolerant, but do not even think of burning their flag. Churchgoers are often quite tolerant of strange doctrines and even outlandish behavior from their clergy, but let the clergy try putting the church flowers in a different spot, and they will discover the power of symbols to arouse passion. In advancing my answer to the first two questions about Jesus—where does he belong within the Judaism of the first century and what were his aims—I am thus developing a pair of answers that will also lay the foundations for answering the next question: Why did Jesus die? I shall argue that Jesus implicitly and explicitly attacked what had become standard symbols of the second-Temple Jewish worldview; he saw them not as bad in themselves but as out of date, belonging to the period before the coming of the kingdom and to be jettisoned now that the new day had dawned. Moreover, the symbols of his own work were deeply provocative, implying at every point that Israel, the people of God, was being redefined in and around him and his work.

Before we get to the detail, we need a further introductory word about Jesus' controversies. Traditional readings of the Gospels have seen Jesus as the teacher of a religion of love and grace, of the inner observance of the heart rather than the outward observance of legal codes. Such readings have then envisaged Jesus being opposed by the Pharisees on the grounds that they believed in a religion of law and outward observances and could not stomach the idea of free forgiveness, of love and grace. This picture, as has been pointed out with increasing frequency in recent years, owes not a little to the Reformation controversies of the sixteenth century, in which the Protestants set themselves up as being in favor of love, grace and the religion of the heart over against the Catholics, whom they saw as propagating a religion of law, merit and outward observances; and also to the worldview of the Enlightenment and/or the Romantic movement, the former highlighting ideas and the latter feelings, both to the detriment of outward and material things and actions.

The great contemporary writer E. P. Sanders has opposed the traditional reading on the grounds of historical implausibility. Jesus, he claims, did not "speak against the law," and what he does seem to have said would not have been particularly irritating to the Pharisees. The key stories in the Gospels, he urges, are made up by the later church and reflect their controversies with later Judaism rather than Jesus' controversies with the Pharisees.

There are many things to be said about this discussion, and I can here only mention some of them. To begin with, traditional form-criticism of the Gospels has grossly overplayed its hand by suggesting that the Gospels reflect the life of the early church rather than that of Jesus. There are many matters of vital concern in the early church that remain unmentioned in the Gospels—circumcision, for instance, or speaking in tongues—and many matters that loom large in the Gospel narratives but that do not seem to have been otherwise prominent in the early church. Furthermore, we do not in fact know as much about later debates between the church and the Jews as some have claimed.

In particular, the picture of Jesus and the Pharisees drawn by Sanders, whose views have become very influential, does not do full justice to the evidence. Let me summarize four key points.[1]

First, the Pharisees were not, as Sanders claims, a small group based only in Jerusalem. In Jesus' time they certainly numbered several thousand, and there is good evidence for their activity in Galilee and elsewhere.

Second, the agenda of the Pharisees in this period was not simply to do with "purity," whether their own or other peoples'. All the evidence suggests that at least the majority of the Pharisees, from the Hasmonean and Herodian periods through to the war of A.D. 66-70, had as their main aim that which purity *symbolized*: the political struggle to maintain Jewish identity and to realize the dream of national liberation. The majority of the Pharisees until A.D. 70 were Shammaites, whose legendary strictness in this period was not simply a matter of the personal application of purity codes but, as we see in the case of Saul of Tarsus, had to do with a desire to purify, cleanse and defend the nation against paganism. The lenient Hillelites, who like Gamaliel believed in living and letting live, did not attain full supremacy until after the two disastrous wars of 66-70 and 132-135 had destroyed the morale of the stricter party.

Third, Sanders is right to stress that these strict Pharisees were not an official "thought police," and indeed that they held, *qua* Pharisees, no post or office. Saul of Tarsus had to get authority from the chief priests for his marauding ventures against the very early church. Nevertheless, this did not stop them as an unofficial and self-appointed pressure group from spying out offenders against Torah. In a passage not discussed by Sanders, Philo speaks of there being thousands of people, "full of zeal for the laws, strictest guardians of the ancestral traditions"—those phrases function in both Philo and Josephus as regular code for the Pharisees—who have their eyes upon transgressors, and are merciless toward those who subvert the laws.[2]

Fourth, Sanders constantly oversimplifies the question by asking, did Jesus or did he not speak against the law? That, however, was not the key issue. If Jesus had simply said that the Torah was redundant, it would indeed be strange to find, as we do, the early church debating about whether Torah was still valid or not. What Jesus did, however, as Sanders recognizes in other areas but not here, was to announce that the new day had dawned, the kingdom was indeed breaking in, and that, as a result, everything would now be different. Paul's discussions about the law are not simply about the question of whether the law is valid or not; they are about the conditions for admitting Gentiles into the people of God, and on that subject Jesus said nothing at all.

What mattered, then, was not religion but eschatology, not morality but the coming of the kingdom. And the coming of the kingdom, as Jesus announced it, put before his contemporaries a challenge, an agenda: give up your interpretation of your tradition, which is driving you toward ruin. Embrace instead a very different interpretation of the tradition, one which, though it looks like the way of loss, is in fact the way to true victory. It was this challenge, I suggest, which when backed up by symbolic actions generated the heated exchanges between Jesus and the Pharisees and resulted in plots against Jesus' life.

The controversies focused not least on the purity codes; but, as I said a moment ago, the purity codes were not simply "about" personal cleanliness, but, as the social anthropologists would insist, were coded symbols for the purity and maintenance of the tribe, the family or the race. Passage after passage in Jewish writers of the period, and indeed in modern Jewish scholarship, emphasizes that the Jewish laws were not designed as a legalist's ladder up which one might climb to heaven but were the boundary-markers for a beleaguered people. Jesus' clash with the Pharisees came about not because he was an antinomian or because he believed in justification by faith while they believed in justification by works but because *his kingdom-agenda for Israel demanded that Israel leave off her frantic and paranoid self-defense, reinforced as it now was by the ancestral codes, and embrace instead the vocation to be the light of the world, the salt of the earth.* I therefore propose that the clash between Jesus and his Jewish contemporaries, especially the Pharisees, must be seen in terms of alternative political agendas generated by alternative eschatological beliefs and expectations. Jesus was announcing the kingdom in a way that did not reinforce but rather called into question the agenda of revolutionary zeal that dominated the horizon of, especially, the leading group within Pharisaism. It is not to be wondered at that he called into question the great emphases on those symbols that had become enacted codes for the aspirations of his contemporaries.

With all this in mind, we can look at the key symbols of Judaism in this period, and begin to understand why Jesus did what he did in relation to them.

Jesus and the Symbols of Judaism
Sabbath. In dealing with the stories of sabbath-controversy (the best

known of which are found in Mark 2:23—3:6), I again take issue with
Sanders and those who have followed him. He regards the stories as
implausible since the Pharisees, he says, did not organize themselves
into groups to hang around cornfields on the off chance of catching
people committing minor transgressions. But again Sanders has gone
back from his basic position, that Jesus was a prophet of Jewish
restoration eschatology. Once we grant that Jesus was at the head of
a movement with an agenda, an agenda moreover clashing with the
Pharisees' agenda, it is entirely credible that a self-appointed group
would take it upon themselves to check up on him. In *Jesus and the
Victory of God* I pointed out, fully aware of the dangers of modern
"parallels," that we have in our own society persons who, though
neither elected nor appointed to positions of public office, take it upon
themselves to scrutinize and criticize those in public life, particularly
if they hold unfashionable opinions. I even suggested that journalists—for it is to them, of course, that I was referring—will go to the
ends of the earth and hide in all kinds of uncomfortable places—not
only Galilean cornfields—in order to acquire compromising photo-
graphs of princesses.[3] What I had not expected when I wrote those
words in 1996 was that a year later camera-wielding journalists would
literally chase a princess, the most famous one of modern times, to her
death. If we suppose that the Pharisees were indeed a kind of religious
"thought police," the Gospel portrait looks farcical. But if we see them
as a self-appointed pressure-group with its own clear agenda, suspicious of alternative movements with rival plans, eager to show up
those with aspirations to a public profile as no better than they should
be, it makes sense not only to see them checking out what Jesus was
up to but making plans to do away with him.

The focus of such activity would be the standard symbols of the
culture and the culture's hopes and aspirations. Did he fly the flag?
Was he a loyal Torah-observant Jew? (Once again we remind ourselves
that this question does not mean, "Did he attempt to justify himself

by works, to earn God's favor by good morals?" but rather, "Did he exhibit those symbolic actions by which the loyal Jew would show gratitude to God?") And among those symbols, as was well-known even among fairly ignorant pagans, one of the chief was the Jewish observance of the sabbath. If today in Jerusalem you are likely to be stoned for driving a car in the wrong part of the city on the sabbath, why should we suppose it unlikely that passions would be roused on the same issue in first-century Galilee?

All the signs are that Jesus behaved with sovereign freedom toward the sabbath. What is more, his justification of his behavior was not such as to quiet suspicion of seditious motives. When challenged (Mk 2:24-28), he responded with a Davidic parallel: David, the true anointed king, was on the run from Saul when he ate the normally forbidden shewbread. The Pharisees were behaving like Doeg the Edomite in 1 Samuel 21, observing what David was up to and then sneaking off to tell. The Son of Man is lord of the sabbath: no doubt there were many to whom that saying remained as cryptic as it does to some contemporary scholars, but there may have been some who heard, beneath the code, the claim that Jesus was the true representative of Israel, at present threatened by the forces of evil but destined to be vindicated by Israel's God.

The two stories in Luke's Gospel about sabbath-breaking emphasize that the sabbath was the most appropriate day for healing to take place.[4] It was the day that signaled release from bondage and captivity. Jesus was indicating that in his view Israel's long-awaited sabbath day was breaking in through his ministry. What was at issue was not "religion" or "ethics" in the abstract. It was a matter of eschatology and agenda. Jesus affirmed Israel's vocation, her belief in her God and her eschatological hope. But this vocation, theology and aspiration were to be redefined around a new set of symbols, appropriate for the new day that was dawning.

Food. Similar points can be made about the complex chapters Mark

7/Matthew 15, where among the points at issue we find the purity laws and particularly the dietary code. Like the sabbath this code functioned in the ancient as in the modern world to mark off Judaism from her pagan neighbors. The key question, once again, was not about petty legalism but about whether Jesus was loyal to the ancestral codes that kept Israel separate from the pagans.

It is vital to grasp that this controversy cannot be projected forward into Mark's day, as though to get Jesus off the hook. Mark has to explain to his readers at the beginning of the chapter what the hand-washing laws are all about; it is very unlikely that this would have been necessary for a church in which serious discussion of the Jewish food laws was a major issue. This conclusion is reinforced by a feature of the narrative that betrays its originality quite clearly. Mark had no need, in his context, to keep Jesus' views on food and purity secret. But he records that Jesus followed, in this case, a regular pattern: a cryptic saying in public, followed by fuller explanation in private (7:14-23). If Jesus had said out on the street that the God-given taboos marking out the Jews from the pagans were now redundant, he might have started a riot. What he was doing was marking, cryptically but definitively, his belief that in the new day dawning Israel was not meant to be keeping God's light all to herself but was to share that light with the world.

Nation and land. In addition to sabbath and food, Jesus placed time bombs beside two other cherished symbols of Israel's identity. Israel's common descent from Abraham and the prohibitions against eating with or intermarrying with Gentiles, while not absolute throughout Judaism in this period, were nevertheless strong enough and are strongly enough attested to make it clear that certain sayings and actions of Jesus would be regarded as deeply subversive. The sense of family identity among the Jews was a central and vital symbol, and some of Jesus' most remarkable sayings seem to be undermining it. "Leave the dead to bury the dead; you go and announce God's kingdom." Ignoring a parent's funeral would be bad enough in our more relaxed Western culture. In Jesus' culture the obligation to bury one's father took precedence even over saying the Shema. Yes, says Jesus, and announcing the kingdom is more important again. Or what about "Who are my mother and brothers?" It is difficult to imagine a young Jewish man saying that in an assimilated modern Western context; in first-century Judaism where family and hence national identity mattered supremely, it is almost unthinkable. "I have come," he says, "to set a man against his family, and a woman against hers." To inherit the age to come one must take leave of family. Jesus is challenging his followers to sit loose to one of the major symbols of the Jewish worldview.[5]

Closely linked with this challenge was the command to abandon possessions. This has usually been read as a kind of proto-monastic challenge, the supreme test of personal devotion. In Jesus' day, and I suggest in Jesus' intention, this command had quite a different overtone. The central possession in that culture was of course land, and the land was another central symbol of Jewish identity.

The challenges to land and family come together in a cryptic passage at the end of Luke 14, along with a double warning about whether Israel is ready to face the crisis that is coming upon her. She is building the Temple for all she is worth, but will it in fact be completed? She is eager to fight a holy war, but will she be able to win it? Jesus is urging his contemporaries to sit loose to the things that had become inalienable symbols of national identity, lest in pursuing the agendas that resulted she would lose all.

This already points to the key symbol, and to Jesus' key action in relation to it. I refer, of course, to the Temple.

Temple. Most contemporary writing about Jesus rightly focuses on the Temple, what Jesus did there and what happened as a result. The Temple was of course, in this period, the heart and center of Judaism, the vital symbol around which everything else circled. It was supposed to be where YHWH himself dwelt, or at least had dwelt and would do so again. It was the place of sacrifice, not only the place where sins were forgiven but also the place where the union and fellowship between Israel and her God was endlessly and tirelessly consummated. It was, not least because of these two things, the center of Israel's national and political life: the chief priests who were in charge of it were also, in company with the shaky Herodian dynasty and under Roman supervision, in charge of the whole nation.

Furthermore, the Temple carried all kinds of royal overtones. Planned by David, built by Solomon, restored by Hezekiah and Josiah, its early history was bound up with the great days of Israel's early monarchy. Zerubbabel had been supposed to rebuild it after the exile; his failure is no doubt closely intertwined with his failure to reestablish the monarchy. Judas Maccabeus and his colleagues cleansed the Temple after the Syrian debacle and thus founded a dynasty that ran for a hundred years—even though they neither had nor claimed any connection with David. Herod's rebuilding of the Temple clearly had more than one eye on the legitimation of his kingship within traditional Jewish categories. Menahem and Simon bar-Giora, two of the would-be messiahs of the war against Rome (A.D. 66-70), presented themselves in public in the Temple before being killed, one by rival Jews, the other by the Romans during Titus's triumph. The last great messiah of the period, Bar-Kochba, had coins minted (this was itself an act of rebellion) on which the Temple façade was pictured. His own intentions, to rebuild the Temple and to establish himself as king, were clear. Temple and messiahship went hand in hand.

At the same time many Jews disapproved of the existing Temple. The Essenes were strongly opposed to the present ruling elite—that, indeed, was the reason why they existed as a separate group in the first place—and hence to the present Temple, the power base of their rivals. They looked for a time when a new Temple would be built, presumably with their own group running it. The Pharisees had already begun to articulate the view that the blessings one normally got by going to the Temple could be had instead by the study and practice of Torah. "If two sit together and study Torah, the Divine Presence rests between them"[6]; this early Rabbinic saying meant that one could have the Temple-privilege of being in the presence of God anywhere in the world. This theology, designed of course not least for Jews in the Diaspora where regular Temple attendance was out of the question, came into its own after A.D. 70 and arguably helped the Pharisees' successors, the Rabbis, to survive and regroup after that great catastrophe. Thus, though the Pharisees were not themselves opposed to the existing Temple, in their thinking it was already relativized; another reason, this, why they scrutinized and criticized Jesus, who was also offering an alternative to the Temple.

Some Jews had a less theological and more socio-economic critique of the existing Temple. There is good evidence that many of the disadvantaged within Judaism saw the Temple as standing for everything that was oppressing them: the rich, corrupt aristocracy and their systematic injustices. A sign of this attitude was the telltale actions of the rebels during the war; when they took over the Temple, they did the ancient equivalent of destroying the central computer in a bank. They burned all the records of debt.

Though Jesus' action in the Temple must naturally be seen within this wider context of disaffection, it goes way beyond it into a different dimension. His attitude to the Temple was not "this institution needs reforming," nor "the wrong people are running this place," nor yet "piety can function elsewhere too." His deepest belief regarding the Temple was *eschatological:* the time had come for God to judge the entire institution. It had come to symbolize the injustice that characterized the society on the inside and on the outside, the rejection of the vocation to be the light of the world, the city set on a hill that would draw to itself all the peoples of the world.

All this forms the context for our own question as to what Jesus himself did in the Temple and what he might have meant by it. There is currently a spectrum of opinion on this question ranging from those who see his action as an attempt to reform or cleanse the system, through to those who see it as an acted parable of destruction. The latter end has been more fruitful, I believe, in recent discussion, but at this point there is still a wide divergence of views: if Jesus' action was a sign of judgment, on what grounds, and with what consequent intent? Sanders, once more, has set up what is already an influential model: Jesus acted out the Temple's destruction because he envisaged that a new Temple would be built, quite possibly by God himself. (We should note that in both ancient and modern Judaism the idea that God will do something, including building the Temple, is not set over against the idea that humans, including architects and builders, may have a hand in the process.)

I have already suggested that, during his Galilean ministry, Jesus acted and spoke as if he was in some sense called to do and be what the Temple was and did. His offer of forgiveness, with no prior condition of Temple-worship or sacrifice, was the equivalent of someone in our world offering as a private individual to issue someone else a passport or a driver's license. He was undercutting the official system and claiming by implication to be establishing a new one in its place. We have also seen that a good deal of Jesus' warning about impending judgment was focused on the Temple. My whole argument so far, in fact, tells strongly in favor of seeing Jesus' Temple-action as an acted parable of judgment. When he came to Jerusalem, the city was not, so to speak, big enough for the two of them together. The central symbol of the national life was under threat, and unless Israel repented it would fall to the pagans. He believed that Israel's God was in the process of judging and redeeming his people, not just as one such incident among many but as the climax of Israel's history. This judgment would take the form of destruction by Rome. It would not (disagreeing with Sanders) be followed by the rebuilding of a new physical Temple. It would be followed by the establishment of the messianic community focused on Jesus himself that would replace the Temple once and for all.

What, then, about the charge: "You have made it a den of thieves" (Mk 11:17)? Does not this indicate that Jesus' primary motive for his attack on the Temple had something to do with economic exploitation? Does it not suggest that he was out to cleanse the Temple, not to symbolize its destruction? Here, as so often, the context of the relevant Old Testament quotation (in this case Jer 7:3-15) is all-important. Jeremiah was not advocating a reform of the Temple; he was predicting its destruction. The Greek word *lēstēs*, here translated "thieves," is in fact the regular word used by Josephus to denote "brigands" or "rebels." When Josephus refers, as he does twice, to "caves of *lēstai*,"[7] he is talking about the literal caves where the desperate revolutionaries used to hide out.

This suggests that Jesus' real charge against the Temple was not that it was guilty of financial sharp practice, though that may have been true as well. As in Jeremiah's day the Temple had become the focal point for the nationalists in their eagerness for revolt against Rome. Even though the people who actually ran it were, as far as the revolutionaries were concerned, part of the problem, the Temple itself was much bigger; it was, they believed, the place where Israel's God had promised to dwell and from which he would defend his people against all comers. How could it then symbolize, as Isaiah had said it should, the desire of Israel's God that it should become the beacon of hope and light for the nations, the city set on a hill that could not be hidden? Jesus saw the present grievous distortion of Israel's vocation symbolized catastrophically in the present attitudes toward the Temple: a symbol that had gone so horribly wrong could only be destroyed. The mountain—presumably Mount Zion—would, figuratively speaking, be taken up and cast into the sea.

Why then, specifically, did Jesus banish the traders from the Temple courts? Without the Temple-tax the daily sacrifices could not be supplied. Without the right money individual worshipers could not buy pure sacrificial animals. Without animals sacrifice could not be offered. Without sacrifice the Temple had—albeit perhaps only for an hour or two—lost its whole *raison-d'être*. Jesus' action symbolized his belief that when YHWH returned to Zion he would not after all take up residence in the Temple, legitimating its present functionaries and the nationalist aspirations that clustered around it and them. Rather, as Josephus realized in a similar context, the cessation of sacrifice meant that Israel's God would use Roman troops to execute upon the Temple the fate that its own impurity and its sanctioning of nationalist resistance had brought upon it. The brief disruption that Jesus effected in the Temple's normal business symbolized the destruction that would overtake the whole institution within a generation.

As with sabbath, food, family and land, so then with Temple. The symbolic actions Jesus performed and the riddling things he said to explain them fill in the picture we have been sketching, the picture of Jesus as a prophet like John the Baptist or Jeremiah, only more so. He was announcing the kingdom of God for which Israel had longed, but it was an announcement that warned of imminent judgment rather than imminent rescue. Let me stress again: I am not saying that Jesus was opposed to the Jewish symbols because he thought them bad, not God-given or whatever. He believed that the time had come for God's kingdom to dawn and that with it a new agenda had emerged diametrically opposed to the agenda that had taken over the symbols of national identity and was hiding all manner of injustices behind them. Jesus, speaking as a prophet in the name and on behalf of Israel's God, declared solemnly in deed and word that the divine judgment was now inevitable. The God who had judged the Temple in the past would now do so once and for all.

Jesus' Symbols of the Kingdom
We now turn our attention to the positive symbols of Jesus' own work.

As I indicated in the previous chapter, there are various things that Jesus did—I instanced his calling of twelve disciples—which spoke volumes about his aims and agenda. We can now fill in this picture with some other details. As Jesus subverted the symbols of land, family, Torah and Temple, so he acted in such a way as to replace these with symbols pointing to his own work and agenda.

Land and people. Jesus seems to have been keenly aware of the symbolism of geographical location. (If we are happy to recognize that the evangelists could think in these terms, it is strange to deny that Jesus could as well.) His choice of key locations for key actions and statements—the Temple and the Mount of Olives are the obvious examples—show that he was well able to take Jewish awareness of symbolic geography and exploit it for his own purposes.

But the biblical texts upon which Jesus seems to have drawn saw the restoration of the land, which was of course part of the whole agenda of the return from exile, as closely bound up with the restoration of broken and damaged human beings. When the wilderness and the barren land were summoned to rejoice, as in Isaiah 35, it was time for the eyes of the blind to be opened, the ears of the deaf to be unstopped, for the lame to leap like a deer and the tongue of the dumb to sing. Jesus' healings, which formed a central and vital part of his whole symbolic praxis, are not to be seen, as some of the early fathers supposed, as "evidence of his divinity." Nor were his healings simply evidence of his compassion for those in physical need, though of course they were that as well. No: the healings were the symbolic expression of Jesus' *reconstitution of Israel.* This can be seen to good effect in the contrast between Jesus' agenda and that of Qumran. Read the so-called "messianic rule" from Qumran (1QSa). There the blind, the lame, the deaf and the dumb were excluded from membership in the community of God's restored people. The rigid—ruthless, one might say—application of certain purity laws meant a restrictive, exclusive community. Jesus' approach was the opposite. His healings were the sign of a radical and healing inclusivism—not simply including everyone in a modern, laissez-faire, anything-goes fashion but dealing with the problems at the root so as to bring to birth a truly renewed, restored community whose new life would symbolize and embody the kingdom of which Jesus was speaking.

Family. Through his actions and words Jesus was calling into being a people with a new identity, a new family. "Here are my mother and my brothers; everyone who hears the word of God and does it" (Mk 3:34-35). This renewed community, a "family" formed around Jesus, included all and sundry, the only "qualification" being their adherence to Jesus and his kingdom-message. This gave to Jesus' message a flesh-and-blood identity that challenged, by implication at least, the groups that adhered to the teaching of the Pharisees or the Essenes. Like a new political party starting up under the nose of the established ones, this was bound to be seen as a threat. But the way Jesus formed and celebrated this new family spoke of God's new world opening up, bringing healing and blessing wherever it went. A powerful combination in a world where power meant danger.

Torah. Along with this symbolic redefinition of the people of God there went certain symbols that seem in Jesus' agenda to have replaced the praxis of Torah as defining characteristics of the restored Israel. In particular we may note the remarkable place given to forgiveness within his teaching. This, once again, should not be seen merely as a particularly difficult ethical challenge. It is a matter, first and foremost, of eschatology. Let me explain by way of a slight detour.

In Jesus' world, as I have stressed, the Jews were longing for the real end of exile. But in the classical prophets and in the books of Ezra, Nehemiah and Daniel, the exile was seen again and again as the result of Israel's sin. When, therefore, Israel longed for the forgiveness of sins, this should not be seen simply in individualistic terms, as the desire for a quiet conscience. When Isaiah 40—55 spoke of YHWH's dealing finally with Israel's sins, what the prophet meant was unambiguous: if the sin that caused the exile had finally been forgiven, the exile would come to an end. Forgiveness of sins was thus a further angle or facet of the eschatological hope. It was first and foremost not so much a state of mind or heart as it was an event.

Jesus' offer of forgiveness, then, was in itself a way of saying that the kingdom was dawning in and through his work. Equally (and this is the point I wish to make here), his *demand* of mutual forgiveness among his followers is not to be seen merely as part of an abstract ethical agenda. It is part of what we might call the eschatological Torah. Jesus' followers were constituted by the fact that he was bringing about the return from exile, the forgiveness of sins. Not to forgive one another would be a way of denying that this great, long-awaited event was taking place; in other words, it would be to cut off the branch on which they were sitting.

This, I suggest, is the explanation of the otherwise astonishingly harsh warnings about those who do not forgive not being themselves forgiven. If Jesus' table-fellowship replaced the food laws, his demand of forgiveness was part of his definition of the new family, the new people of God. In other words, it was part of his redefined symbolic Torah. As such, though there is no space to develop this further here, it rightly belonged at the heart of the prayer that he gave to his disciples, the prayer that, as many scholars have pointed out, itself formed a key part of the symbolic praxis of Jesus' followers, defining them over against other movements within Judaism, claiming for them the status of being the kingdom-people, the forgiveness-people, the true sons and daughters of Israel's God.

Temple. When we allow these positive symbols to generate a larger picture of Jesus' intentions, we find once again that the focal point of it all is the Temple. There are several indications in the Gospels that Jesus was deliberately acting in such a way as to say that where he was and where his followers were, Israel's God was present and active in the same way as he normally was in the Temple. This, as will be apparent, meant that his agenda stood in parallel to that of the Pharisees. Alternatives like that are threatening.

Consider, to begin with, the question of fasting. The difference between Jesus' disciples and those of John and the Pharisees, in the little exchange in Mark 2:18-22, has nothing to do with "patterns of religion." It was not (as is often suggested) that the two groups who practiced the outward observance were interested only in externals while Jesus was interested in the heart. Fasting for Jews in this period was not simply an ascetic discipline. It had to do with Israel's present condition—she was still in exile. More specifically, it had to do with the destruction of the Temple.[8] Zechariah (8:19) had promised that the days of fasting, which commemorated the Temple's destruction, would be turned into feasts, but this could only come about, obviously, when YHWH restored Israel's fortunes and more specifically caused the Temple to be properly rebuilt, something that Zechariah, like other "post-exilic" prophets, was very concerned about. That is what Jesus was meaning in speaking of the wedding guests not being able to fast while the bridegroom was with them. The party—the messianic banquet, symbolized in Jesus' celebratory feasts—was in full swing, and nobody wants glum faces at a wedding. God was now doing what he had promised. The great blessings of exile's end, YHWH's return and the rebuilding of the Temple were now happening, for those with eyes to see.

If, then, we inquire as to Jesus' attitude to the dominant symbols of the Judaism of his day and as to his own chosen symbols, we find that Temple and Torah dominate the landscape, as we would expect. In relation to both, Jesus stood within Israel's noble tradition of critique from within. The critique was sharp. Israel's present appropriation of her national symbols was leading her to ruin. Jesus was warning of this in the clearest way possible, while at the same time inviting all who would do so to repent and come with him in his way of being Israel.

All the lines of investigation I have followed to this point lead the eye up to two great symbolic actions. One we have already studied and will return to: Jesus' critique of the Jewish symbol-system led to his action in the Temple. One I have not yet mentioned. If we wanted to draw together the positive symbols of Jesus' own work and to sketch a single picture in which they all feature, we might do worse than to envisage this young kingdom-prophet celebrating with his twelve closest disciples the greatest of Israel's feasts, the feast that spoke most clearly of liberation, exodus, covenant and forgiveness. If the negative symbols embodying Jesus' critique of his contemporaries come together in the Temple-action, the positive symbols of Jesus' work come together in the upper room. And with that we are poised to consider the central questions that will occupy us in the next chapter.

Conclusion

By way of conclusion and summing-up of the last three chapters, let me offer three reflections on where we have got to so far.

First, in the light of all that I have said, we should not be surprised to find evidence that one regular reaction to Jesus was that he was "leading the people astray." Judaism was well-equipped with categories for people who came along with alternative teachings, offering signs and wonders to turn Israel away from loyalty to the ancestral traditions. The false prophet, the rebellious elder, the rebellious son—there is evidence that each of these accusations was at some time or another launched against Jesus. In particular, the later rabbinic memory of Jesus was that he was a magician who acted as a false prophet; this may well go back to one feature of the trial before Caiaphas.[9]

Second, we should now be able to address and solve one of the oldest questions about the kingdom of God.[10] From the point of view of his ministry, did Jesus regard the kingdom as present or future? Once we locate him on the map of first-century Judaism, alongside other kingdom-movements, prophetic movements and messianic movements, the answer is obvious. If you had asked Bar-Kochba in, say, A.D. 133 whether the kingdom was present or future, he would have said, "Both." To deny that it was present would be to deny that he was the true leader, appointed to bring about Israel's redemption. If it was not present, why did he put the year 1 on his coins? Equally, to deny that it was future would have been ludicrous. The kingdom would not be complete until the Romans were defeated and the Temple rebuilt. Once we realize that the kingdom of God was not just about religion and ethics but about eschatology and politics and the theology that holds them all together, some of the longest-running scholarly debates can be shown to be beside the point.

Finally, what can we say about the first two questions we set ourselves? Where does Jesus belong in relation to Judaism, and what were his aims and goals? I have argued that Jesus remained utterly anchored within first-century Judaism. His place there, however, was the place of a prophet, warning that Israel's present course was leading to disaster and urging a radical alternative upon her. His aim was to reconstitute the people of God around himself, to accomplish the real return from exile, to inaugurate the kingdom of God. This would not happen, however, simply by repetition of his message and his symbolic actions until more and more people were persuaded. It would come about through the decisive events to which his two great symbolic actions pointed. The Temple-action spoke of messiahship; the Last Supper pointed to the cross. It is to this strange combination of ideas, more deeply meaningful but more deeply subversive within first-century Judaism than all we have so far seen, that we must now give our attention.

CHAPTER FOUR

THE CRUCIFIED MESSIAH

S O FAR I HAVE PAINTED A PICTURE OF JESUS OF NAZARETH AS A PROPHET announcing the kingdom of God. This involved him in a radical critique of the Judaism of his day and in a radical summons to his hearers to follow him in what amounted to a new way of being Israel. From this point of view we cannot avoid the double question that will occupy us in this chapter: "Did Jesus think of himself as Messiah, and if so in what sense?"[1] and, "Did Jesus expect or intend to die as part of his vocation, and if so what interpretation did he put upon that event?"[2]

Three important preliminary points: Few if any first-century Jews imagined for a moment that the Messiah would in any sense be divine. When Peter is reported to have said, "You are the Christ," and when Caiaphas asked, "Are you the Christ?" neither of them was thinking of trinitarian theology. So, too, the phrases "son of God" and "son of man" carried messianic connotations, in some circles at least, in the Judaism of this period, but they did not in themselves refer to a divine being. The question, whether Jesus thought he was the Messiah, and indeed the different question, whether he *was* in fact the Messiah, are not the same as the question, whether he was or thought he was in any way the embodiment of Israel's God. Let us take one thing at a time. Delayed gratification again.

Second, it is high time to abandon the reticence, masquerading as prudence but in fact consisting only of timidity, which has prevented scholars from allowing Jesus to be (what we would call) a thinking, reflective theologian. We have learned in the last generation that not only Paul, John and the author of Hebrews, but also Matthew, Mark and Luke were highly gifted, reflective and creative theologians. Why should we be forced to regard Jesus as an unreflective, instinctive, simplistic person, who never thought through what he was doing in the way that several of his contemporaries and followers were well able to do?

Third, we may note that in attempting to understand Jesus' sense of his own vocation we are not attempting to study his psychology. It is hard enough to get clear information about the psychological state of someone in our own culture who answers all our questions in our own language. To suppose one can achieve results with someone from a different time and culture is to go blindfold into a dark room to look for a black cat that probably isn't there. What we can in principle do as historians, however, is to study someone's *awareness of vocation*. We can do this with Paul or John the Baptist. We can even do it, to some extent, with the emperor, Augustus. We can certainly do it with the self-congratulatory Cicero. A recent book has attempted to do it with the shadowy figure of the "Teacher of Righteousness" who left his mark on the Dead Sea Scrolls.[3] We can examine their actions and sayings and can work back with a fair degree of certainty to their aims and intentions. This is not to psychoanalyze them. It is to do what historians normally do.

So, then, what did second-Temple Jews think about the Messiah? It is important to recognize from the start that there was no single unified concept of the Messiah in the first century. The idea of kingship itself is wider than that of texts that speak of a Messiah; we must factor in Israel's actual experience and expectations of kings, whether Hasmonean or Herodian. Where royal hopes were cherished, it was not in isolation but rather as the sharp edge of the hope of the nation as a whole, the hope for liberation, for the end of exile, for the defeat of evil, for YHWH to return to Zion. And the coming King would do two main things, according to a variety of texts and as we study a variety of actual would-be royal movements within history. First, he would build or restore the Temple. Second, he would fight the decisive battle against the enemy. David's first act upon being anointed was to fight Goliath; his last was to plan the Temple. Judas Maccabeus defeated the Syrians and cleansed the Temple. Herod defeated the Parthians and rebuilt the Temple. Bar-Kochba, the last would-be Messiah of the period, aimed to defeat the Romans and rebuild the Temple. The messianic agenda aimed, through these things, to do for Israel what Israel's prophets had declared would be done: to rescue Israel and to bring God's justice to the world. Part of asking, "Did Jesus think he was the Messiah?" is to ask, "Did he in any sense intend to accomplish these tasks?"

It is unlikely that the followers of a crucified would-be Messiah would regard such a person as the true Messiah. Jesus did not rebuild the Temple; he had not only *not* defeated the Romans, he had died at their hands in the manner of failed revolutionary leaders. Israel was not rescued; pagan injustice still ruled the world. However, the belief that Jesus was the true Messiah is deeply and ineradicably embedded in the very earliest Christianity for which we have any evidence, so that already by the time of Paul the word *Christos* has attached itself to the name Jesus in several different formulae. The early Christians continued to use this word with its royal overtones even when it was embarrassing and dangerous to do so. The question presses: Why?

The answer cannot simply be: Because of the resurrection. Within the world of second-Temple Judaism, not even resurrection would have generated the belief that the newly alive person was the Messiah unless people had already at least suspected that he was that prior to his death. If, for instance, one of the seven brothers martyred in 2 Maccabees 7 had been raised to life three days after his horrible torture and death, people would have said the world was a very odd place; they would not have said that he was the Messiah. We must take seriously, then, the fact that Jesus was crucified as a would-be Messiah—as the "title" on the cross itself indicates!—and that the resurrection thus affirmed, to Jesus' surprised followers, that he was after all Messiah, even though the crucifixion had seemed to disprove the claim. We are thus forced back to ask: What evidence is there during Jesus' ministry that he launched in any sense a messianic claim?

Jesus and Messiahship

The best and most obvious evidence is found in Jesus' action in the Temple. This, as I argued in the previous chapter, should be understood not as an attempt at reform but as an acted symbol of judgment. But who has the authority to pronounce the Temple's judgment? The answer is, the King, acting on God's behalf. The so-called "triumphal entry" into Jerusalem and the action in the Temple are full of royal overtones. The most recent parallel in the history of Israel had of course been the action of Judas Maccabeus, coming into Jerusalem with palm branches waving (2 Macc 10:7) as part of defeating the pagans and restoring the true worship in the sanctuary. That was the basis for Judas's family to mount a royal dynasty that lasted a century. Jesus' action must be seen as implying a similar royal claim.

The symbolic action is eloquent in itself, but by no means stands alone. Here we see one of the great advantages in working from actions to sayings, as against the attempt to decide upon authentic sayings first and leave the actions for later. Jesus' messianic Temple-action is surrounded with several sayings that function, as it were, as royal riddles, explaining, sometimes cryptically, the meaning of what had just happened. Among these royal riddles we here have space to examine only three (Mark 11:27—12:12, 35-37).

First, the question about authority. By what authority is Jesus doing these things? What right has he got to behave in this apparently messianic fashion, and where did he get this right from? Jesus' reply, asking his interlocutors what they thought of John the Baptist, is not simply a difficult counterquestion to get himself off the hook. It is a cryptic answer to the question. Throughout the synoptic tradition Jesus refers to John as the last great prophet, the Elijah who is to come; but if John is Elijah, that means that Jesus must be at least the Messiah. More specifically, there seems to be a reference to John's baptism as the time when Jesus was anointed with the Spirit for his new task: when, in other words, he became the anointed one, the Messiah.

This interpretation is confirmed by the fuller riddle, this time a parable, which follows immediately. The story of the Wicked Tenants is precisely a story about a line of rejected prophets, culminating in the rejected Son. The parable, like so many, tells the story of Israel, culminating in judgment, but it also includes the story of Jesus within it. The tenants who reject the son will incur judgment just as Jesus has announced, and now enacted, judgment upon the city and Temple which have rejected his message. The parable thus serves as a further explanation of Jesus' action.

The parable runs straight into the additional riddling remark about the son and the stone. "The stone which the builders rejected has become the head of the corner" (Mk 12:10). This is a quotation from Psalm 118, a pilgrim psalm about building the Temple, celebrating in the Temple and ultimately sacrificing in the Temple. Jesus is claiming to be building the eschatological Temple. What is more, in the vision of Daniel 2 the stone that is cut out of the mountain, which smashes the idolatrous statue and then itself becomes a kingdom filling the whole earth, was regularly interpreted messianically; in addition, some first-century readers of Daniel seem to have made the punning connection, in Hebrew, between the stone *(eben)* and the son *(ben)*.

Thus the story of the rejected servants climaxes in the rejected son; he, however, is the messianic "stone" that, rejected by the builders, takes the chief place in the building. Those who oppose him will find their regime (and their Temple) destroyed, while his kingdom will be established. The whole riddle serves as a further and richer explanation of what Jesus had done in the Temple and why.

The third messianic riddle to be considered here is the question Jesus asks his interlocutors concerning David's Lord and David's son (Mk 12:35-37). How, he asks, can the Messiah be David's son, when according to Psalm 110 he is also David's Lord? This has sometimes been understood as a denial of Jesus' Davidic messiahship, but this is certainly wrong. An apparently better suggestion is to see it as a redefinition of what Davidic messiahship actually means, specifically that Jesus would be opposing current speculations about a coming warrior king. But it would be strange to use Psalm 110, a very militaristic psalm, for this purpose. Rather, I suggest that the point of the question is twofold. First, this psalm goes on to insist that the king is also "a priest for ever, after the order of Melchizedek"; he therefore has authority over the Temple, so that the question functions as a further oblique explanation of what Jesus had been up to. Second, this psalm, particularly the verse quoted here, revises the messianic portrait *so that it includes an enthronement scene*, in which the one enthroned will act as judge. Jesus is once again affirming his right to announce the doom of the present Temple and its ruling elite. By posing the question the way he has, Jesus is both cryptically affirming his claim to be David's true son and also pointing to the larger claim, that he carries the authority of David's Lord. About this we shall have more to say in the next chapter.

These riddles find a natural home within the proclamation of Jesus himself. The same is true, I suggest, of the passage that follows almost immediately, namely, the so-called apocalyptic discourse of Mark 13 and parallels, at which we glanced in chapter two. Suffice it to note here that this passage, too, carries clear messianic overtones, not least through Jesus' use of the phrase "son of man" in reference to himself. In the first century as Josephus, 4 Ezra and other texts show, the picture of the Son of Man who is vindicated after his suffering at the hands of the beasts was readily taken by some Jews to refer to the coming King.[4]

This will also help when we consider that most controversial of topics, the so-called Jewish trial of Jesus in Mark 14:53-65. It has long been customary, even traditional, to read Mark's scene of Jesus before Caiaphas as a succession of *non sequiturs* reflecting nothing in the life of Jesus but rather the much later theology of the early church. Indeed, even to question this is, as I have discovered in some academic circles, to call down upon oneself the anathemas that used to be reserved for theological heretics.

Once we read the larger story in the way I have suggested, however, the passage gains a new coherence. Caiaphas asks Jesus about his Temple-action; this was the natural starting point since we may suppose that this action was the proximate cause of Jesus' arrest. When Jesus offers no reply, Caiaphas asks him directly whether he is the Messiah; this, once we grasp the nexus of Temple and Messiah, is of course the obvious next move. Jesus' answer is to be read as a basic affirmative, reinforced with a double biblical quotation from two passages that have already been significant in his messianic riddles: Psalm 110 and Daniel 7. "You will see the Son of Man sitting at the right hand of Power, and coming on the clouds of heaven." In other words, Caiaphas will witness Jesus' vindication in the events following Jesus' death and in the judgment that will fall upon his regime and its central symbol. This final declaration thus not only answers the question about Messiahship but also explains what Jesus had intended in his Temple-action and the riddles surrounding it. It also explains, without more ado, how it was that the chief priests were able so easily to hand Jesus over to the governor on the charge of being a rebel king and how it was that Pilate came to crucify Jesus with the words "King of the Jews" inscribed above his head.

Historically, this sequence makes perfect sense. It explains, finally, why Jesus was regarded as Messiah by his followers after his resurrection. And once we see this whole picture starting to develop, we can see also that many features of Jesus' public career before his arrival in Jerusalem fit into the same pattern. Among evidence not often noted in this context, there are several passages where Jesus seems about to come into conflict with Herod, the present claimant to be the King of the Jews. There are also interesting texts from Qumran that alert us to messianic links we might not otherwise make.[5] Jesus' regular celebrations of feasts with his motley group of followers can best be seen as a symbolic enactment of the messianic banquet, and once again, a good many riddles and smaller sayings point in the same direction. He had believed all along, it seems, that it was his vocation to be Israel's Messiah; only in Jerusalem did this veiled claim come out into the open and then more in symbolic actions than in spoken teaching. Once we place the Temple-action in the center of the discussion and work outward from there, we can be confident in arguing that Jesus had seen himself as Messiah since at least his baptism by John and that his work in both Galilee and Jerusalem, though carrying most obviously the hallmarks of a prophetic ministry, had the note of messiahship as a constant subtext.

It was, of course, a redefined notion of messiahship, cognate with Jesus' whole doubly revolutionary redefinition of the kingdom of God itself. Jesus seems to have believed himself to be the focal point of the real returning-from-exile people, the true kingdom-people; but that kingdom, that people and this Messiah did not look like what the majority of Jews had expected. Jesus was summoning his hearers to a different way of being Israel. We now have to come to terms with the fact that he believed himself called to go that different way himself as Israel's anointed representative and to do for Israel—and hence also for the world—what Israel could not or would not do for herself.

Jesus' redefined notion of messiahship corresponded to his whole kingdom-proclamation in deed and word. It pointed on to a fulfillment of Israel's destiny that no one had imagined or suspected. He came as the representative of the people of YHWH to bring about the end of exile, the renewal of the covenant, the forgiveness of sins. He came to accomplish Israel's rescue, to bring God's justice to the world.

But how was this to be done? One might expect, granted the pattern of other messianic and similar groups within Judaism, an agenda such as the following: that he should go to Jerusalem, wage the war against the forces of evil and be enthroned as God's Messiah, Israel's true King. There is a sense in which this is exactly what Jesus did. But it was not the sense that his followers expected.

The Crucifixion of the Messiah

Jesus' belief in his vocation to messiahship is, I suggest, one of the main clues that can help us understand his sense of vocation vis-à-vis the cross. This question logically includes, of course, the question as to why the Romans actually executed him and why the Jewish authorities handed him over to them. But for brevity's sake I want to focus on the question of Jesus' own intentionality.

Let me introduce this theme with a story. When I was a professor at McGill University, Montreal, in the early 1980s, I taught a sixth-grade Sunday-school class in our local church. I once began a class by asking them the question: "Why did Jesus die?" They thought about it with no conferring, and we then went around the room and collected single-sentence answers. The interesting thing was that about half of them gave me historical reasons: he died because he upset the chief priests; he died because the Pharisees didn't like him; he died because the Romans were afraid of him. The other half gave me theological answers: he died to save us from our sins; he died so that we could go to heaven; he died because God loves us.

We spent a fascinating hour putting those two sets of answers together. I do not know if any of those children remember that session, but I certainly do. I still believe that this putting together of the two sides of that great question—the historical dimension and the theological one—is one of the most important tasks we can engage in when studying Jesus.

Here perhaps more than anywhere else we run into major problems of historical description of two sorts in particular. First, though I cannot argue this here, I suggest that the sources, despite of course being written from a particular point of view and replete with theological interpretation, give us nevertheless easily enough historical material to be going on with. Second, there has been considerable discussion as to whether Jesus went to Jerusalem intending to die there or at least knowing that it was likely and making no attempt to avoid this fate. Here again we run into the distinction between Schweitzer and Wrede. Wrede, followed by most twentieth-century scholars, dismissed the idea that Jesus expected or even intended to die. Schweitzer, by putting Jesus into his eschatological and apocalyptic Jewish context, discovered that there was then a way of making sense of Jesus' strange intentionality. My proposal has considerable affinity with Schweitzer's, though with certain corrections, developments and additions.

We begin once again with a central symbolic action. One of the great Jewish scholars of our day, Jacob Neusner, has argued recently that what Jesus did in the upper room was designed to balance and complement what he did in the Temple.[6] Though I disagree with Neusner as to the exact meaning of these actions, I think in essence he is correct. The two actions, in the Temple and in the upper room, are, as I argued in the previous chapter, the climax of two strands of activity in Jesus' public career. Jesus' action in the Temple brought his challenge to the prevailing symbolic world to its climax. The Temple was the greatest Jewish symbol, and Jesus was challenging it, claiming authority over it, claiming for himself and his mission the central place the Temple had occupied. The Last Supper was Jesus' own alternative symbol, the kingdom-feast, the new-exodus feast. And, just as the Temple pointed to the sacrificial meeting of the covenant God and his people, the sign of forgiveness and hope, of God dwelling in their midst as the God of covenant renewal, covenant steadfastness, covenant love, so now Jesus by his double action was claiming that here, in his own work, in his own person, all that the Temple had stood for was being summed up in a new and final way.

What then can we say about the Last Supper?

The meaning of a Passover meal is not controversial. It is, of course, debated as to whether the Last Supper *was* a Passover meal; I have become convinced that it was, even if, consonant with Jesus' other subversive practices, he celebrated it on the wrong night. Passover linked the feasters with the exodus, not merely by way of long-range memory but by constituting them again as the liberated people, the covenant people of YHWH. Celebrating Passover at any time since the Babylonian exile would have the immediate and obvious meaning that the feasters were also celebrating, in faith and hope, the real end of exile, the renewal of the covenant. And since one of the key meanings of the return from exile would be that Israel's God had at last forgiven the sins that sent her into exile in the first place, a Passover meal in the second-Temple period spoke powerfully in itself, before any words were said, of that forgiveness of sins, the eschatological blessing of new covenant.

In celebrating this quasi-Passover meal with his fictive kinship group, his twelve followers, Jesus seems to have intended a further level of symbolic meaning, again before any words were spoken. If the story of Israel was reaching its climax, as the meal indicated, it would do so through him and his fate. His actions with the bread and the cup, like Ezekiel's actions with a brick and Jeremiah's with a smashed pot, functioned as prophetic symbolism, pointing to the actions of judgment and salvation that he believed YHWH was about to accomplish. In this context the words that he spoke suggest that Jesus was deliberately evoking the whole exodus-tradition and indicating that the hope of Israel would now come true in and through his own death. His death, he seems to be saying, must be seen within the context of the larger story of YHWH's redemption of Israel; more specifically, it would be the central and climactic moment toward which that story had been moving. Those who shared the meal with him were the people of the renewed covenant, the people who received "the forgiveness of sins," that is, the end of exile. Grouped around him, they constituted the true eschatological Israel.

How might this reading of the Last Supper make sense within an overall interpretation of Jesus and his intention? We have already seen that Messiahs were supposed to fight Israel's great battle against the old enemy and rebuild the Temple as the place where YHWH would meet with his people in grace and forgiveness. But as we recall from the previous chapters, Jesus' challenge to his contemporaries was that they should engage in the doubly revolutionary program through which Israel would become the light of the world, not through fighting military battles but through turning the other cheek and going the second mile. At the heart of Jesus' subversive agenda was the call to his followers to take up the cross and follow him, to become his companions in the alternative kingdom-story he was enacting. My proposal is that Jesus took his own story seriously. He would himself travel the road he had pointed out to his followers. "He would turn the other cheek; he would go the second mile; he would take up the cross. He would be the light of the world, the salt of the earth. He would be Israel for the sake of Israel."[7] He would defeat evil by letting it do its worst to him.

Once we get the point, we can see what is going on in the various riddles that once again surround the central symbolic action. Again, I choose only three. Luke records in 23:31 a strange saying as Jesus goes to the cross: "If they do this when the wood is green, what will they do when it is dry?" The context—a warning to the women of Jerusalem about the judgment that will come upon themselves and their children—evokes various biblical prophecies about the coming destruction that would result from the city refusing her true king and turning away from the way of peace. Jesus seems to have been saying that his own death at the hands of the Romans was the clearest sign of the fate in store for the nation that had rejected him. Rome had condemned him on a charge of which he was innocent but of which a good many of his compatriots were thoroughly guilty. He was the green tree, they the dry.

We should note that the saying does not carry any sort of atonement-theology such as characterized the church's understanding of Jesus' death from very early on. It belongs not with the earliest post-Easter reflections on the crucifixion but on the lips of Jesus himself. It suggests that Jesus understood his death as being organically linked with the fate of the nation. Having announced YHWH's judgment on Temple and nation alike, Jesus was now going ahead to undergo the punishment that symbolized the judgment of Rome on her rebel subjects.

This theme comes into further prominence in the second riddle. "How often," said Jesus, "would I have gathered you as a hen gathers her chicks under her wing, and you would not. Behold, your house is left desolate."[8] This, too, is a warning of judgment upon the God-forsaken Temple. But the image of hen and chicks again indicates Jesus' intention vis-à-vis that judgment. The picture is of a farmyard fire; the hen gathers her chicks under her wings, and when the fire has run its course, there will be found a dead hen scorched and blackened, but with live chicks under her wing. Jesus seems to be indicating his hope that he would take upon himself the judgment that was hanging over the nation and city. It suggests that he, like Elijah in Sirach 48:10, had hoped to turn away the divine wrath from Israel. But the chance had come and gone. Jesus' fate remains indissolubly locked together with that of Jerusalem, but she has chosen not to benefit from his work.

The third riddle comes in Jesus' answer to James and John. Can they drink the cup that he will drink or be baptized with the baptism he is to be baptized with?[9] The "cup," which occurs again in the Gethsemane narrative, denotes suffering or even martyrdom, and in prophetic writings is frequently the cup of YHWH's wrath. The "baptism" seems to refer to a fate that Jesus still has to suffer, to which the baptism of John, with its exodus-symbolism, would be the appropriate pointer. Jesus will share the fate of Israel so that the true exodus may come about.

As we allow these riddles—which I have treated here only in the very briefest form—to interpret the central symbolic action in the upper room, a picture starts to emerge. Jesus seems to have regarded his own approaching death as being part, indeed the climax, of the vocation in which his work and Israel's fate were bound up together. In the light of this, we can make sense of the so-called passion predictions punctuating the synoptic narrative at various points.[10] By themselves, their authenticity is regularly challenged, but if we begin with the Last Supper and work back through the explanatory riddles, a framework emerges within which they make a good deal of sense.

That sense, moreover, finds its home, as Albert Schweitzer saw a century ago, within the context of second-Temple Jewish beliefs about the coming eschatological redemption. Within the controlling story of exile and restoration we find in several biblical and post-biblical texts a major subplot: the deliverance will come about through a time of intense suffering, sometimes referred to as the "messianic woes." The great tribulation would burst upon the nation and through it redemption, the new age, the forgiveness of sins, would come about. Schweitzer argued that Jesus saw this time of testing, the *peirasmos*, coming upon Israel and that his intention was to take it upon himself. Hence his command to the disciples to watch and pray lest they, too, should enter the *peirasmos*. This gains extra credibility when we consider the ways in which some Jewish groups and individuals thought of themselves as becoming the focal points of Israel's suffering: the Maccabean martyrs, various of the prophets and the righteous man who in Wisdom of Solomon 2—3 is persecuted and killed but will be vindicated. Similar themes can be traced at Qumran.[11]

All these second-Temple developments seem to go back to various biblical texts: Daniel, the Psalms, Zechariah, Ezekiel and of course Isaiah, particularly the servant passages in Isaiah 40—55. I do not think that second-Temple Jews had already abstracted a "servant-figure" out of this latter book or had developed a particular theology of atonement or redemption around such a figure; rather, all these writings bear witness to a sense that Israel's sufferings as a nation would be focused at a particular point. There was, that is to say, no such thing as a straightforward pre-Christian Jewish belief in an Isaianic "servant of YHWH" who, perhaps as Messiah, would suffer and die to make atonement for Israel or for the world.

> But there was something else, which literally dozens of texts attest: a large-scale and widespread belief, to which Isaiah made a substantial contribution, that Israel's present suffering was somehow held within the ongoing divine purpose; that in due time this period of woe would come to an end; that the explanation for the present state of affairs had to do with Israel's own sin; that the present suffering would somehow hasten the moment when Israel's tribulation would be complete, when she would finally have been purified from sin, so that the exile could be undone. There was, in other words, a belief, hammered out not in abstract debate but in and through poverty, torture, exile and martyrdom, that Israel's sufferings might be, not merely a state *from* which she would, in YHWH's good time, be redeemed, but paradoxically, under certain circumstances and in certain senses, be part of the means *by* which that redemption would be effected.[12]

My argument is that Jesus and his self-understanding as he faced death are to be located in the middle of this worldview.

I propose, in other words, that we can credibly reconstruct a mindset in which a first-century Jew could come to believe that YHWH would act through the suffering of a particular individual in whom Israel's sufferings were focused; that this suffering would carry redemptive significance; *and that this individual would be himself.* And I propose that we can plausibly suggest that this was the mindset of Jesus himself. Let me show how this works out, step by step.

Jesus believed that Israel's history had arrived at its focal point. More specifically, he believed that the *exile* had reached its climax. He believed that he was himself the bearer of Israel's destiny at this critical time. He was the Messiah who would take that destiny on himself and draw it to its focal point. He had announced the judgment of YHWH on his recalcitrant people; now as with the prophets of former days they were planning to kill him. Jesus had declared that the way to the kingdom was the way of peace, the way of love, the way of the cross. Fighting the battle with the enemy's weapons meant that one had already lost it in principle and would soon lose it and lose it terribly, in practice. Jesus determined that it was his task and role, his vocation as Israel's representative, to lose the battle on Israel's behalf. This would be the means of Israel's becoming the light, not just of herself—the Maccabean martyrs seemed only to think of Israel's liberation—but of the whole world.

Like those martyrs, Jesus suffered what he saw as the results of Israel's pagan corruption:

> Israel had flirted with paganism; suffering would come of it, as it always did; the martyrs took it upon themselves. Unlike them, Jesus saw as a pagan corruption *the very desire to fight paganism itself.* Israel had become a hotbed of nationalist revolution; suffering would come of it, specifically in the form of Roman swords, falling masonry, and above all crosses planted outside the city wall. He would go, as Israel's representative, and take it upon himself. As in so many of his own parables, he would tell Israel's well-known story one more time, with a radical and subversive twist in its tail. Only he would tell it, not as a wordsmith,

swapping aphorisms in the market-place, but as the king, exiled outside
the gate of his own beloved city.[13]

He would thereby do for Israel what Israel could not do for herself.
He would fulfill Israel's vocation that she should be the servant
people, the light of the world.

This, I suggest, was how Jesus understood his messianic vocation.
The Messiah, as we have seen, was expected to rebuild or cleanse the
Temple and to fight Israel's great battle. How did Jesus see his own
vocation in relation to these tasks?

He would not rebuild the Temple in a physical sense. He would
become the place and the means whereby that for which the Temple
stood would become a reality. He would be the reality to which the
sacrificial system had pointed. He had regularly, throughout his ministry, acted in such a way as to bypass the Temple and its system,
offering forgiveness to all and sundry on his own authority. He now
went to his death, indicating in his last great symbolic action that a
way was being opened through which that normally obtained by the
sacrificial system was now to be obtained through him.

More especially, he would fight the messianic battle. He had
already laid down its terms: he who saves his life will lose it, but he
who loses his life will gain it. Instead of the insults and threats that
the martyrs had hurled at their accusers, Jesus, as the entire many-
sided early Christian tradition bears witness, suffered in silence,
except for words of forgiveness and hope. This is so remarkable an
innovation into the martyr-tradition that it is quite inexplicable unless it is true to the historical facts. Having been known for his
remarkable compassion throughout his public work, Jesus' last great
act drew into one that giving of himself for others to which the early
church referred so regularly and with such awe.

I have elsewhere drawn together the long and complex argument
about Jesus' intentions in these words, upon which I do not think that
I can presently improve:

Jesus, then, went to Jerusalem not just to preach, but to die. Schweitzer was right: Jesus believed that the messianic woes were about to burst upon Israel, and that he had to take them upon himself, solo. In the Temple and the upper room, Jesus deliberately enacted two symbols, which encapsulated his whole work and agenda. The first symbol said: the present system is corrupt and recalcitrant. It is ripe for judgment. But Jesus is the Messiah, the one through whom YHWH, the God of all the world, will save Israel and thereby the world. And the second symbol said: this is how the true exodus will come about. This is how evil will be defeated. This is how sins will be forgiven.

Jesus knew—he must have known—that these actions, and the words which accompanied and explained them, were very likely to get him put on trial as a false prophet leading Israel astray, and as a would-be Messiah; and that such a trial, unless he convinced the court otherwise, would inevitably result in his being handed over to the Romans and executed as a (failed) revolutionary king. This did not, actually, take a great deal of "supernatural" insight, any more than it took much more than ordinary common sense to predict that, if Israel continued to attempt rebellion against Rome, Rome would eventually do to her as a nation what she was now going to do to this strange would-be Messiah. But at the heart of Jesus' symbolic actions, and his retelling of Israel's story, there was a great deal more than political pragmatism, revolutionary daring, or the desire for a martyr's glory. There was a deeply theological analysis of Israel, the world, and his own role in relation to both. There was a deep sense of vocation and trust in Israel's god, whom he believed of course to be God. There was the unshakable belief—Gethsemane seems nearly to have shaken it, but Jesus seems to have construed that, too, as part of the point, part of the battle—that if he went this route, if he fought this battle, the long night of Israel's exile would be over at last, and the new day for Israel and the world really would dawn once and for all. He himself would be vindicated (of course; all martyrs believed that); and Israel's destiny, to save the world, would thereby be accomplished. Not only would he create a breathing space for his followers and any who would join them, by drawing on to himself for a moment the wrath of Rome and letting them escape; if he was defeating the real enemy, he was doing so on behalf of the whole world. The servant-vocation, to be the light of the world, would come true in him, and thence in the followers who would regroup after his vindication. The death of the shepherd would result in YHWH becoming king of all the earth. The vindication of the "son of man" would see the once-for-all defeat of evil, the rescue of the true Israel, and the establishment of a worldwide kingdom.

Jesus therefore took up his own cross. He had come to see it, too, in deeply symbolic terms: symbolic, now, not merely of Roman oppression, but of the way of love and peace which he had commended so vigorously, the way of defeat which he had announced as the way of victory. Unlike his actions in the Temple and the upper room, the cross was a symbol not of praxis but of passivity, not of action but of passion. It was to become the symbol of victory, but not of the victory of Caesar, nor of those who would oppose Caesar with Caesar's methods. It was to become the symbol, because it would be the means, of the victory of God.[14]

Conclusion

I have experienced two negative reactions to the material in this chapter, both as I have presented it in lectures and as people have read the similar statements that I have made in print. On the one hand, people regularly say that it sounds very strange and peculiar. Some Christians, used to the apparently straightforward theology of hymns like "There is a green hill far away" and the easy-to-grasp presentation of certain types of atonement-theology, find it all very complex and difficult. How can we conceive that Jesus really thought all those things, and what does it do to our simple faith if we think he did? Equally, some critical scholars have chided me with claiming to know more than we can and with projecting back into Jesus' mind all sorts of things that we cannot be sure were ever there.

To the latter I say, not for the first time, that the best historical hypothesis is the one that with appropriate simplicity explains the data before us, and that, since so many details of this picture are *not* the same as the early church's atonement-theology, while they nevertheless offer themselves as the root from which that theology could have grown, a very strong case can in fact be made out, which is not to be wished away by the mere repetition of scholarly dogma ("we know that Jesus couldn't have thought such things"). First-century Jews demonstrably *did* think within that world, and all the signs are that Jesus did indeed make this particular construal of the overarching narrative and apply it to himself.

To the former I say, not for the last time, that the way to Christian growth is often to allow oneself to be puzzled and startled by new apparent complexity. There is great simplicity at the heart of this picture, but it is costly. The price it demands is sustained attention to the specific, and to us strange and perhaps even repellent, first-century ways of thinking that characterized Jesus. Is it after all Jesus we want to discover and follow, or would we prefer an idol of our own making?

Four comments in conclusion. First, all this of course is only of any abiding relevance if we say that Jesus of Nazareth rose again from the dead. I shall come to the question of Easter in chapter six. For the moment, we should note that if Jesus' body had stayed in the tomb there is no explanation for why anyone would have taken seriously his claims to messiahship, or to a particularly meaningful death, for a single moment after his execution. Crucified Messiahs, as everybody knew, were failed Messiahs. So what, they might have thought, if Jesus did cherish grandiose and complex, perhaps even very pious, beliefs about his own approaching liquidation? He's more the fool for that. No, without the resurrection all of this is just so much whistling in the dark. It is Easter that validates Jesus' interpretation of his own death.

Second, the cross, seen as I have said in the light of Easter, offers itself as the great turning-point of history. If we are to follow Jesus' own understanding of his vocation, it was the moment when the evil and pain of all the world were heaped up into one place, there to be dealt with once and for all.

This, of course, challenges us acutely with the question: Why then do evil and pain still seem to be so rampant in the world? It is

somewhat comforting to notice that the early Christians, who made
the claim about the efficacy of the cross as starkly as anyone, faced the
same problem. Colossians and Ephesians, where Paul celebrates the
achievement of Jesus so magnificently, are written from prison, as the
principalities and powers still have their way with him. This is a
tension we are to live with; though we should note that if the victory
of the cross is not worked out in the life of the world, if it is to be
confined only to the so-called "spiritual" sphere, we are implicitly
denying part of Jesus' own meaning. It means, of course, that this
interpretation of cross and resurrection demands that we also believe
in a yet-to-come final consummation, when God will wipe away all
tears from all eyes. All this points on to the final two chapters in the
present book.

Third, the cross can be seen as Jesus' final great act of love. It draws
to a climax all those actions throughout his ministry—his touching of
a leper, his tenderness toward the chronically sick or bereaved, his
tears at Lazarus' grave—in which we see the deeply human, and (as
I shall argue in the next chapter) characteristically God-filled Jesus
truly at work. When John declares that Jesus, having loved his own
who were in the world, now loved them to the uttermost (Jn 13:1), this
is not a later theological spin being overlaid on top of events that were
originally not like that at all. This is simply telling it like it was.

Fourth, I want to highlight again, from this new vantage point in
our story, the place to which we have come in facing "the challenge of
Jesus" in terms of the tasks that await us in our world. When we speak
of "following Christ," it is the crucified Messiah we are talking about.
His death was not simply the messy bit that enables our sins to be
forgiven but that can then be forgotten. The cross is the surest, truest
and deepest window on the very heart and character of the living and
loving God; the more we learn about the cross in all its historical and
theological dimensions, the more we discover about the One in whose
image we are made and hence about our own vocation to be the

cross-bearing people, the people in whose lives and service the living God is made known. And when therefore we speak (as did the conference from which this book sprang) of shaping our world, we do not—we dare not—simply treat the cross as the thing that saves us "personally," but which can be left behind when we get on with the job. The task of shaping our world is best understood as the redemptive task of bringing the achievement of the cross to bear on the world, and in that task the methods, as well as the message, must be cross-shaped through and through. To this we shall return in the final chapters.

In my experience, though, there are two other questions that press upon people when they have followed the argument this far. What did Jesus believe about himself and God? And what precisely happened at Easter? These will occupy us in the next two chapters.

CHAPTER FIVE

JESUS
& GOD

I HAVE BECOME USED TO BEING ASKED, AFTER LECTURING THROUGH THE material covered so far, the questions: first, "Was Jesus God?" and second, "Did Jesus know he was God?" These are urgent and important questions, but they need redefining before they can be addressed.[1]

The problem is that the word *god* or *God* simply does not mean the same thing to all people who use it; and, what is more, most people in Western culture today, when they use the word, do not have in mind what mainstream, well-thought-out Christianity has meant by it. The result is quite drastic: if I were simply to answer yes to either of the questions I just mentioned, the majority of my hearers would hear me affirming something I do not believe to be true. I do not think that Jesus thought he was identified with the being that most people in our culture think is denoted by the word *god*.

What most people mean by *god* in late-modern Western culture is the god of Enlightenment Deism. That far-off, detached being may perhaps have been responsible in some sense or other for the creation of the world, but he—or perhaps one should say "it"—is basically remote, inaccessible and certainly not involved with the day-to-day life, let alone the day-to-day pain, of the world as it now is. Even to think of "divine intervention" is, in these terms, a category mistake; such a god would not dream of "intervening." Of course, many Christians, anxious to retain a theoretical base for their sense of God's presence and power, have, while speaking of God as utterly detached from the world, also spoken of the same God as intervening "miraculously" within the world—saying, in effect, that though it should not logically happen, God is greater than logic and so can, as it were, break his own rules. But this is not how the Bible speaks of God. And it is, even more importantly, not the vision of God that we discover in Jesus.

At the same time there has been a resurgence of interest in our post-secular world in all kinds of vaguely "religious" or "spiritual" matters. Bookshops produce ever larger sections on "spiritual growth," with sections on reincarnation, "channeling," Feng Shui, discovering one's personal goddess and other apparently enticing topics. "Spirituality" and "divinity" have, it seems, come back with a bang—as long as they have nothing to do with anything like mainstream Christianity, which is usually represented in the same bookshops by a selection of white-bound Bibles and Prayer Books, designed to be confirmation presents and, one may safely assume in 95 percent of the cases, destined to be left to gather dust on a shelf. (Aside from that, some of the larger bookstores, particularly in the United Kingdom but often in the USA as well, will stock lurid books of the "Jesus-was-an-Egyptian-Freemason" type but not so often the equally readable and ultimately far more satisfying books that explore the actual historical origins and contemporary meaning of genuine Christianity.)

There are, then, plenty of "gods" currently on offer. But do any of them have anything to do with Jesus? It is vital that in our generation we enquire once more: to what, or rather whom, does the word *god* truly refer? And if as Christians we bring together Jesus and God in some kind of identity, what sort of an answer does that provide to our question?

When I was younger, the answers on offer to these questions posed stark alternatives. On the one side many Christians were content with some form of the argument advanced by C. S. Lewis in many writings. Jesus claimed to be divine; this means that he was either mad (which the rest of his teaching belies) or a deliberate crook (which his whole life and particularly his death tells strongly against) or he was telling the truth, and we must swallow it. On the other side one was told repeatedly by theologians at what seemed the highest level that all this was simply nonsense. We knew as a matter of certainty that it was absurd for God to be human or for a man to be divine. The categories were mutually exclusive. No sane person could think themselves to be divine (a line of thought advanced by the American theologian John Knox in the 1950s and repeated ad nauseam in certain circles ever since). More particularly, no first-century Jew could think of himself as in any sense "divine"; Jews were after all monotheists, and the idea of a human somehow being divine could only be a later idea, a pagan corruption of the original, nonincarnational thinking and teaching of Jesus and indeed of the early church. Appearances to the contrary were dealt with in short order: the "claims" of Jesus to "divinity" were, it was said, inventions from the end of the first Christian generation or later, read back, not least in John's Gospel, onto the lips of Jesus.

These two positions appeared to the theological students of the 1960s and 1970s a long way apart. The battle between them was not hand-to-hand fighting; the lines were drawn up some distance from each another, like North Parade and South Parade, a mile or more apart in North Oxford, leaving an uncomfortable no man's land between the Royalist and Parliamentarian troops in the English Civil War. Cannons fired from a distance allowed both sides to tell their supporters that they had won a victory. Those who ventured into the space in between tended to be shot at by both sides.

Sometimes, long after a war is over, some soldiers are still hiding in the jungle, unaware that the world has moved on to other matters. Two such soldiers chancing to meet might still fight to the death, but their contest would be irrelevant in terms of the new world situation. This, I think, is the situation of many who are still fighting the war between the confident assertion that Jesus claimed to be God, and so must have been, and the equally confident assertion that he could not have been, so he could not have claimed to be and was not. At the risk of incurring the wrath of both sides I must beg leave to disagree. The world has moved on, and it is history—the study of first-century Judaism and Christianity in particular—that has moved it. There are new battles not totally different, of course, from the old ones but with significant new elements. Also, I believe, there are significant new possibilities for reconciliation.

"God" in First-Century Judaism

The key starting point must be to get inside the minds of Jesus' Jewish contemporaries on this question: What did they mean by the word *god?*

Some theologies believe in a god or gods but think of this being or these beings as quite separate from our world. They are distant and remote, happy in their own sphere not least because they have little or nothing to do with ours. Others believe that god, or "the divine," or "the sacred," is simply one aspect, one dimension, of our world: "god" and the world end up being pretty much the same thing, or at least *god* becomes a way of referring to the sense of wonder, of spiritual possibility, latent within the world as we know it.

Both of these views can be the starting point for an eventual atheism: either the theoretical sort (where people think their way to unbelief) or the practical sort (where people have nothing to do with the god/gods in whom they profess to believe). The first type simply allows its "god" get so far away that he disappears; this is what happened in some thinkers of the nineteenth century who allowed the "distant god" of Deism to drift off like a stray satellite that finally ceases to orbit the earth and becomes lost forever in outer space. The second type can get so used to acknowledging various divine "forces" personified into different "gods" that they become commonplace and trivial, acknowledged only in occasional superstitions. This is what happened with a good deal of ancient paganism in Greece and Rome.

Equally, both of these views can give birth to (or are they actually caused by?) the currently fashionable relativism. It is an interesting observation on today's religious climate that many people now get every bit as steamed up about insisting that "all religions are just the same" as the older dogmaticians did about insisting on particular formulations and interpretations. The dogma that all dogmas are wrong, the monolithic insistence that all monolithic systems are to be rejected, has taken hold of the popular imagination at a level far beyond rational or logical discourse. The "remote god" view encourages it: if god is, or the gods are, far away and largely unknowable, all human religions must be at best vague approximations, different paths up the mountain (and all the paths get lost in the mist quite soon anyway). Equally, the pantheism that sees "god" as the divine or sacred aspect within the present world leads ultimately in the same direction: if all religions are responding to "the sacred" in this sense, they are simply different languages expressing the same concept.

Few who embrace one or other of these beliefs (or in some cases, it seems, both) stop to consider how remarkably arrogant and imperialistic these rejections of the supposedly arrogant and imperialistic religions actually are. They are saying with all the authority of the eighteenth-century Enlightenment behind them that they have discovered the hidden truth that all the great religions (especially Judaism, Christianity and Islam) had missed: all religions are "really" variations on the Enlightenment's idea of "religion." Well, of course: if you start with that idea, it would look like that, would it not?

But why should we believe the Enlightenment's arrogant claim any more than anyone else's? Some Christians, thinking to be generous-spirited toward those who embrace different faiths, have spoken of such people as "anonymous Christians"; this is now generally rejected as hopelessly arrogant. Why should a Buddhist want to be an "anonymous Christian?" But by the same token it is just as arrogant, if not more so, to claim that the adherents of *all* religions are really "anonymous Enlightenment religious persons."

We cannot, obviously, settle this huge debate here. I merely raise it to show the way in which different ideas of "god" give rise to or are raised by various current ideas about the meaning of the world and of the religions. And also to show that the Jewish idea of "God" was quite different both from the distant, remote being(s) of ancient Epicureanism and more recent Deism, and from the immanent god(s) of ancient and modern paganism and pantheism.

The Jews believed in a specific God, of whom there was only one, who had made the whole world and who was present to it and active within it while remaining sovereign over it and mysteriously other than it. They knew this God (though at some point they stopped saying this name) as YHWH, "the One Who Is," the Sovereign One. He (they used masculine pronouns for YHWH, though they knew very well that he was beyond gender, and they could often use feminine imagery as well) was not remote or detached. Nor was he simply a generalized sense of a sacred dimension within the world or for that matter the objectification or personification of forces and drives within the world. Rather, he was the *maker* of all that exists and remained powerful and involved within, though by no means reduced to terms of, the creation itself. Classic Jewish monotheism thus came to believe that (a) there was one God, who created heaven and earth, and who remained in close and dynamic relation with his creation; and that (b) this God had called Israel to be his special people. This latter vocation was sometimes explicitly linked with the former belief: YHWH had chosen Israel *for the sake of* the larger world. Election, the choice of Israel, was the focal point of the divine purpose to act within the world to rescue and heal the world, to bring about what some biblical writers speak of as "new creation."

This twin belief (monotheism and election; or, if you prefer, creation and covenant) was never simply a pair of abstract propositions arrived at by philosophical enquiry or hypothetical speculation. It was discovered through a particular history and characteristically expressed through telling and retelling that history in one shape or another. The history was that of Abraham's family going down into Egypt, becoming enslaved and being dramatically rescued and given their own land. Those who lived through these events explained who they were and gave shape to their continuing life by telling the story and dramatically reenacting it in various festivals. Whatever happened subsequently, whether oppression, suffering, exile or seeming annihilation, the family of Abraham looked back to the story of the exodus to rediscover who their God was and to pray that he would do for them once more those acts that had constituted them as his people in the first place.

Part of the story was precisely the discovery of what God's faithfulness and rescuing power would look like in practice—or to put it another way, what the strange name of God, YHWH, might actually mean (Ex 6:2-8). This God would be known as the rescuer, the one who would then accompany his people through the wilderness, leading them in the pillar of cloud and fire, and giving them his law, his own self-expression of the way of life for his people. The story of the exodus thus included within itself the story of two ways in which the one true God was present and active within the world and Israel: the "Shekinah," the glory of God "tabernacling" within the tent in the wilderness and later within the Temple in Jerusalem; and the Torah, the expressed will of God for Israel, the law of Moses. In addition, a strong strand in the story was the belief that God's own Spirit had rested upon and indwelt Moses (and some of his colleagues), enabling him to be the leader of God's people. These three manifestations of YHWH's presence and rescuing love—God's presence, God's law, God's Spirit, all seen to great advantage in the rescue-story, the freedom-story, that is, the Exodus narrative—mark off the Jewish sense of who their God actually was from the theologies of the surrounding nations.

In many places in the Jewish Scriptures and in subsequent post-biblical Jewish writings these three ways of thinking about God's presence and saving activity, within the world and within Israel, were linked closely with two others: God's Word and God's Wisdom. Both are associated with creation; both are seen as other ways of saying what was said through Shekinah and Torah. Together these five ways form, not indeed a philosophical system, but a controlling narrative. Through retelling and reliving this story in liturgy and festival, in reading, singing and prayer, Israel was able to rekindle the sense of God's presence. She was able to root herself again in YHWH's rescuing actions in the past; to pray, often in extreme circumstances, for his rescuing help in the present; and to hope for his final victory and her own final liberation from all that enslaved her, in the future.

Into this Jewish picture of the one true God we must now factor two other features characteristic of some Jewish writings in the second-Temple period. First, there was the expectation of the return of YHWH to Zion after his abandonment of Jerusalem at the time of the exile. Second, there was the tradition of the enthronement of YHWH, and of one who somehow shared that throne. There is a good deal to be said about both, but constraints of space demand that this account be brief.[2]

YHWH's return to Zion is a major theme of the exilic and postexilic Old Testament books. It is central to Isaiah, particularly chapters 40—55 and the developing theme, there, of the kingdom of God. Ezekiel, the prophet who declared most emphatically that YHWH had abandoned his people to their fate, envisages him returning to the newly built eschatological Temple. The Psalms celebrate the coming of YHWH to judge the world. Haggai, faced with the puzzling second Temple that failed to live up to expectations, envisages YHWH returning to a yet more glorious house. Zechariah employs exodus-imagery—the pillar of cloud and fire—to express the way in which YHWH will return to dwell with and defend his people, and offers an apocalyptic scenario in which YHWH will come with all his holy ones to become king of all the earth, reigning from Jerusalem. Malachi promises that the Lord whom Israel seeks will suddenly come to his Temple, even though his coming will bring judgment as well as salvation.

But the geographical return from exile, when it came about under Cyrus and his successors, was not accompanied by any manifestations such as those in Exodus 40, Leviticus 9, 1 Kings 8 or even Isaiah 6. Never do we hear that the pillar of cloud and fire that accompanied the Israelites in the wilderness has led the people back from their exile. At no point do we hear that YHWH has now gloriously returned to Zion. At no point is the house again filled with the cloud that veils his glory. At no point is the rebuilt Temple universally hailed as the true restored shrine spoken of by Ezekiel. No new festival was invented to mark the start of the great new era. Significantly, at no point either is there a final decisive victory over Israel's enemies or the establishment of a universally welcomed royal dynasty. Temple, victory and king-ship remained intertwined, but the hope they represented remained unfulfilled. It is therefore not surprising that the scriptural tradition that refers unambiguously to YHWH's return to Zion after the exile is maintained in the postbiblical writings. This expectation remained basic to Judaism in the time of Jesus.

If YHWH were to act in history and if he did so through a chosen agent, how might that chosen agent be described? This is the second aspect of first-century Jewish thinking that helps us understand the context of Jesus' symbolic act and the stories and riddles with which he surrounded it.

According to some texts from our period, when YHWH acted in history, the agent through whom he acted would be vindicated, exalted and honored in a quite unprecedented manner. This is a separate subject in itself, and I must be content with pointing in a general direction with some specific instances.

There is a complex range of Jewish texts from different periods that speculate about the exaltation and the heavenly enthronement of a figure who may be either an angel or a human being. These speculations grow from meditation upon and discussion of certain key texts such as Ezekiel 1, in which the prophet receives a vision of YHWH's throne-chariot, and Daniel 7, where "one like a son of man" is presented to "the Ancient of Days" and shares his throne. Such speculations formed the staple diet of a whole tradition of Jewish mysticism and accompanying theological and cosmological enquiry.

Sometimes the texts speak of a mystical journey, of people attempting to attain to the vision of the one true God himself. Sometimes they speak of an angel who has the name of Israel's God dwelling in him. Sometimes they speak of a human being sharing the throne of Israel's God. Several strands of tradition tell the story of Moses in this fashion; some even speak thus of the martyrs or the pious. In one famous story that occurs in various forms and periods the great rabbi Akiba suggests that the "thrones" spoken of in Daniel 7:9 are "one for God, one for David." Akiba, of course, had a candidate in mind: Bar-Kochba, whom he hailed as the Messiah, "the son of the star." Other Jewish teachers of the same period seem to have speculated on the possibility of a plurality of "powers" within "heaven."

How far these speculations were taken is a matter of continuing debate. But the point should be clear: things like this were thinkable; they were not obviously self-contradictory, nor were they regarded as necessarily a threat to what second-Temple Jews meant by "monotheism." They were attempts to find out what that monotheism actually meant in practice. Thus, out of a much larger and highly complex set of speculations about the action of Israel's God through various mediator-figures, one possible scenario that some second-Temple Jews regarded as at least thinkable was that the earthly and military victory of the Messiah over the pagans would be seen in terms of the enthronement-scene from Daniel 7, itself a development of the chariot-vision in Ezekiel 1.

One thing should be clear from this brief survey of first-century Jewish beliefs about the meaning of the word *God* (or perhaps we should say about the character and activity of YHWH). Jewish monotheism was much more complicated than was supposed by those who said so glibly that since Jews were monotheists they could not conceive of a human being as divine. Equally, it should be clear that to pick up a few phrases from John's Gospel and elsewhere and to claim on the basis of them that Jesus simply "claimed to be divine," is far too simplistic and may well by implication buy in to similarly misleading views of what "divinity" might actually mean. The way forward is more complex but ultimately far more rewarding than the old battle lines would suggest.

Early Christian Views of Jesus and God

All the signs are that the earliest Christians very quickly came to the startling conclusion that they were under obligation, without ceasing to be Jewish monotheists, to worship Jesus. An older assumption, that this could only have happened insofar as they abandoned their Judaism and allowed pagan ideas to creep in surreptitiously, must now be abandoned. The evidence for the phenomenon I am describing is very early, very solid and quite unambiguous.

I have described elsewhere in considerable detail the way in which Paul and quite possibly traditions that were already well-known by the time he was writing, speaks of Jesus not only in the same breath as speaking of the one God of Jewish monotheism but actually *within* such statements. The key passages are 1 Corinthians 8:1-6, Philippians

2:5-11, Galatians 4:1-7 and Colossians 1:15-20, though once the point is grasped one can see further evidence of the same phenomenon, clear if not so striking, in many other places in his writings.[3] There should be no question of Paul in these passages or elsewhere moving away from the Jewish monotheism we know in biblical and postbiblical sources and into either paganism, which would allow further "gods" to be added to a pantheon, or dualism, in which the good God would be opposed to a bad god, the redeemer (perhaps) over against the creator. For Paul, "there is one God (the Father, from whom are all things and we to him), and one Lord, Jesus Christ (through whom are all things and we through him)" (1 Cor 8:6). This stunning adaptation of the Jewish prayer known as the *Shema* ("Hear, O Israel, the LORD our God, the LORD is One" [Deut 6:4]), emphasizing creation and redemption as equally originating in the Father and equally implemented through Jesus, encapsulates, at the earliest stage of Christianity for which we have hard evidence, everything that later generations and centuries would struggle to say about Jesus and God. From here on, we must say that if trinitarian theology had not existed it would be necessary to invent it. That, in fact, is effectively what the first generation of Christians did, worshiping Jesus within the framework of Jewish monotheism.[4]

But where did this all begin? Where on earth did they get the idea that they should do this? Does it in any sense go back to Jesus himself? That is the key question at the heart of the present chapter, and we are now very nearly in a position to address it.

Very nearly, but not quite. We must first identify and head off three false trails.

The first two I have already mentioned.[5] It is commonly supposed among Christians and non-Christians alike that the word *Messiah* carries connotations of "divinity," so that if Jesus is shown to have thought of himself as Messiah, that means he thought of himself as divine. This is simply not the case. The would-be Messiahs of second-

Temple Judaism did not, so far as we know, think of themselves in this way, nor did their followers attribute divinity to them. If Bar-Kochba is an exception, as I hinted earlier, he appears as a radical innovation (leaving Christianity itself out of the equation) within the tradition. And, since the phrase "son of God" in this period functioned as a messianic title, it did not carry in and of itself the overtones of "divinity" that later Christian theology would hear in it. (The transition from a purely messianic meaning to a Messiah-plus-incarnation meaning begins in the New Testament, not least in the passages I mentioned a moment ago; it may go back to Jesus himself, as we shall see; but it cannot be read out of the phrase itself within its Jewish context.)

The third false trail is the resurrection, which I shall deal with in the next chapter. Again and again one hears it suggested that the resurrection somehow proves Jesus' divinity, so that to affirm or deny the one is to affirm or deny the other. This mistake goes easily with the previous one, for instance in the misreading of Paul's phrase that Jesus was marked out as "son of God" through the resurrection (Rom 1:4); what Paul meant was that Jesus was publicly designated *Messiah* through that event. Nothing in the Jewish expectation of resurrection indicates that anyone would conclude that, faced with someone alive again with a new sort of life following death, such a person must be in some sense divine. To the contrary: resurrection was what was supposed to happen to all the dead, or at least all the righteous dead, and there was no suggestion that this would simultaneously constitute divinization. No: the resurrection awoke the dejected disciples to the truth that Jesus was in fact the Messiah; from this they concluded both that he was indeed the Lord of the world, as the Messiah was always supposed to be, and that his death, rather than being a shameful defeat, was in fact the strange but glorious victory over all the forces of evil. From this combination of beliefs they went on forward into the unknown to declare that since Jesus had thus accomplished the mighty saving act that could only be the personal work of YHWH, the God of the exodus, Jesus was somehow to be identified as the personal manifestation, the embodiment, of the one God of Israel. The resurrection was essential for this train of thought to be begun, but it did not in and of itself "mean" that Jesus was therefore divine.

The resurrection, establishing Jesus as Messiah, did however link in to one particular biblical prophecy that was important within some strands of second-Temple Judaism, that became equally important within early Christianity and that points interestingly to a way of understanding Jesus' sense of his own identity, which I and others have found helpful. In a well-known and indeed classic passage, David enters into a dialogue with YHWH. David intends to build a house for YHWH, so that instead of the wandering tent left over from the wilderness period YHWH can live in a proper, fixed house.[6] There are all sorts of overtones to this, of course, not least David's desire to consolidate his own rule and power and the status of his new capital, Jerusalem, within all the tribes of Israel. It may be partly for this reason that the response comes back via the prophet Nathan that David is not to build him a house, but the crucial thing is that the offer of a house is turned inside out. YHWH will build David a house; only it will not be a house of fine timber, stone and paneling (he already has one of those), but a "house" in the sense of a *family*. More specifically, YHWH will give David a son who will be king after him, and this son will build a Temple for YHWH to live in. What is more, YHWH will adopt him as his own son.[7]

The crucial verse for the present point is 2 Samuel 7:12. When David dies, then, declares YHWH, "I will raise up your seed after you, who will sit on your throne." The Hebrew for "I will raise up" has no particular connotations at the supposed time of writing of "resurrection." But when the Old Testament was translated into Greek some two or three hundred years before the time of Jesus, the verse was rendered *kai anastēso to sperma sou*, "I will resurrect your seed." Since it was at roughly this time that Jewish beliefs in the resurrection of the dead had started to blossom, it is fair to suppose that perhaps the translators and certainly those Jews who read 2 Samuel in this version saw the passage as a prophecy that God would raise David's true and ultimate "seed" from the dead and that this resurrected "seed" would be, in some new sense, God's own son.

This still does not bring us, however, all the way to the key point. What we now have to do is to reflect, admittedly with early Christian hindsight, on the significance of God's response to David. David was offering to build a timber-and-stone house as a dwelling place for God. God's response was that this was secondary; what mattered was that he, God, would build a "house" for David consisting ultimately of David's son who would be God's son. And, suggested the Septuagint translation, this son would be known by being raised from the dead.

Read this story now with early Christian eyes, and what do we find? That the Temple, for all its huge importance and centrality within Judaism, was after all a signpost to the reality, and the reality was the resurrected son of David, who was the son of God. God, in other words, is not ultimately to dwell in a human-built Temple, a timber-and-stone house. God will indeed dwell with his people, allowing his glory and mystery to "tabernacle" in their midst, but the most appropriate way for him to do this will not be through a building but through a human being. And the human being in question will be the Messiah, marked out by resurrection. This, I submit, is more or less how the early Christians reasoned. Jesus—and then, very quickly, Jesus' people—were now the true Temple, and the actual building in Jerusalem was thereby redundant. We must remind ourselves, crucially, that the Temple was, after all, the central "incarnational" symbol of Judaism. It was standard Jewish belief, rooted in Scripture and celebrated in regular festivals and liturgy, that the Temple was the place where heaven and earth actually interlocked, where the living

God had promised to be present with his people.

With this we are ready at last to move back to Jesus himself. What signs are there within his own agenda and vocation that these trains of thought originated with him rather than being wished on him by the early church?

The Vocation and Self-Understanding of Jesus

Central to all that follows is the argument that Jesus, at the very center of his vocation, believed himself called to do and be in relation to Israel what, in Scripture and Jewish belief, the Temple was and did. If, therefore, Judaism did indeed have a great incarnational symbol at its very heart, namely the Temple, then for Jesus to upstage the Temple, to take on its role and function and to legitimate this with Davidic claims, meant that Jesus was claiming that he rather than the Temple was the place where and the means by which the living God was present with Israel.

This argument is in some ways easier to mount by working backward from the events of the last week of Jesus' life to the hints earlier in the ministry. But to keep the length of this chapter down as far as may be in the hope that readers will want to follow up the argument and work it out further for themselves, we may begin with one of the central features of Jesus' itinerant ministry. He offered people "forgiveness of sins," not only by saying so but also in some of his most characteristic actions, namely, his welcome to and his feasting with "sinners" of all sorts. He offered, in other words, the blessing that was normally obtained by going to, or at least (in the Diaspora) praying toward, the Temple. The immensity of this should not be missed. It was not merely a democratization of the Temple-cult; there is a sense in which the Pharisees offered that too, urging that when one studied Torah, wherever one might be at the time, one was just as much in God's presence as when one went to the Temple (see below). Rather, it was the offer of the new-covenant reality to which the Temple was the old-covenant signpost. That which you might obtain at the Temple—and would then need to obtain again after another round of sinning and impurity—you could have now and forever by accepting Jesus' welcome, by trusting in him, by following him. He was the personal embodiment of what the Temple stood for.

The apparent exception proves the rule.[8] When Jesus tells the healed leper to go and show himself to the priest and to make the offering Moses commanded for a proof of the cure, the reason should be obvious. It is not that Jesus was submitting to the superior authority of the Temple. The cure had already been effected. But the leper needed to be readmitted into ordinary social life in the village, and if he simply told his family and friends that he had been pronounced "cured" by a strange wandering would-be prophet, they might well have remained unconvinced. What he needed for reintegration into his social world was the official rubber stamp of the recognized authorities. But in the other cases—the blind receiving their sight, the lame being cured, and so on—there was no need for anything further to be done. The cure was obvious.

These actions and the forgiveness and welcome that they symbolized were part of the wider total ministry of Jesus. His kingdom-announcement, which we looked at in chapters two and three, carried at its heart the claim that Israel's God was even now present and active in the new way that had long been promised and for which Israel had been waiting. His refusal to fast on the days commemorating the Temple's destruction indicated, however cryptically, that he saw his own work as in some sense the building of the new Temple. His implicit opposition to the house of Herod (see, for instance, Mt 11:2-15), offering himself as the true king of the Jews in place of what he and many others saw as a parody of Jewish kingship, was opposition to the house that, in succession to the Maccabean regime, was rebuilding and beautifying the Jerusalem Temple as part of its attempt to legitimate itself as the true royal house of Israel. His solemn and

often-repeated warnings about the fate of Jerusalem in general and
the Temple in particular raised the question not only of who he
thought he was to pronounce such judgment (a prophet? the Messiah?) but also of what he thought YHWH would put in its place. As
soon as we ask that question, Jesus' answer should be obvious. YHWH
would not build a new building to replace the old one (as seems to be
envisaged in, for instance, the Qumran scrolls). YHWH would replace
the entire system with the new community that consisted precisely of
Jesus and his people.

All this meant—and this meaning is heavy with incarnational
significance—that when Jesus came to Jerusalem there was bound to
be a confrontation between himself and the Temple. The city, the
system, was simply not big enough for the two of them to coexist.
There could not be, ultimately, two places, two means, for the one God
to dwell with his people and to do so in forgiving and restorative love,
reaching out to the world as always intended. Jesus' critique of the
Temple was sharp, and there were many corruptions within the
Temple-system of his day that caused other Jews to be angry with its
rulers and the way it was run; but he was going beyond specific
critique to eschatological confrontation. When the reality appears,
what happens to the signpost?

Jesus' action in the upper room, therefore, takes on more significance when we see it as in some ways his own alternative to the
Temple-cult. It follows his demonstration in the Temple with the
symbolic enactment of that which would replace the building and all
that it stood for: the celebration of the new exodus, in which he himself
would lead his people through the ultimate Red Sea and off to the
Promised Land. Nor was Jesus merely being the new Moses. He was
acting as if it were his vocation to be the pillar of cloud and fire, leading
the people to freedom.

My conclusion from this brief survey of the evidence is that Jesus
believed himself called to act as the new Temple. When people were

in his presence, it was as if they were in the Temple. But if the Temple was itself the greatest of Israel's incarnational symbols, the conclusion was inevitable (though the cryptic nature of Jesus' actions meant that people only gradually realized what he had in mind): Jesus was claiming, at least implicitly, to be the place where and the means by which Israel's God was at last personally present to and with his people. Jesus was taking the huge risk of acting as if he were the Shekinah in person, the presence of YHWH tabernacling with his people.

In the light of all this we can look much more briefly at the other four symbols by means of which Jews of the period thought of YHWH's being present and active amongst them and indeed in the world as a whole.

First, Torah. As Jacob Neusner has strikingly shown, the way in which Jesus managed to upstage the Mosaic Torah in his teaching (notably, but by no means only, in the Sermon on the Mount) indicates that he regarded himself as authoritative over Torah and authorized to issue a new version of it in a way that made him not a new Moses but in some sense or other a new YHWH.[9] Torah, too, certainly by the time of Jesus, was (to use the not inappropriate shorthand) an incarnational symbol for Judaism: it was not only the word from God but the living presence of God's word with and for the people of Israel. For someone to announce and embody a new Torah, in continuity with the old to be sure but going strikingly beyond it in various respects (Mt 5:17-20), was to make the implicit claim that in his teaching and in his presence as teacher, the living God was somehow present. This is the claim that is then summed up in a saying attributed to Jesus, which has a remarkable parallel in a (probably later) rabbinic saying. "Where two or three gather in my name," declares Jesus, "there am I in the midst" (Mt 18:20). "Where two sit together and words of the Law are spoken between them," declared Rabbi Hananiah ben Teradion, "the Shekinah rests between them."[10] That saying almost certainly originates in the period after the destruction of the Temple and points to the way in which Torah could be the means of YHWH's presence for a people who would otherwise be bereft of it. Jesus' saying acts simultaneously as an upstaging both of Torah and Temple. Meeting "in his name"—presumably what is envisaged is a cell of Jesus' followers in a particular village where he had been—is equivalent to studying Torah; his presence with them is equivalent to the presence of YHWH in the Temple.

The same is true, more briefly still, of the other God-language used in Judaism. "The sower sows the word";[11] Jesus' ministry is understood as a manifestation of the word of God, the creative, healing, restorative word evident in the creation of the world and promised by the prophets as the means of the great coming restoration.[12] Jesus heals "with a word," and this is remarked upon as a sign of his astonishing personal authority.[13] Likewise, Jesus acts by the Spirit: "If I by the Spirit of God cast out demons, then the kingdom of God has come upon you."[14] And the language of his teaching constantly evokes that of the true Wisdom, subverting conventional wisdom with the call to trust in God and act accordingly; only now Wisdom seems to consist in hearing Jesus' words, believing his eschatological message, and acting on it.[15]

The Synoptic Gospels thus bear witness, albeit cryptically, to Jesus' reuse in relation to his own work of the five ways in which the Judaism of his day spoke of the presence and activity of YHWH within the world. This must be set, of course, within the larger context of his eschatological preaching, his announcement that the kingdom was breaking in through his own work; and when we do this we discover that these hints find an appropriate home. They are, in fact, the tips of the iceberg. Jesus in his entire public career was acting as if he were bringing about the new exodus. God's people were in slavery; he had heard their cry and was coming to rescue them. Just as the first exodus revealed the previously hidden meaning of YHWH's name, so now

Jesus would reveal the person, one might say the personality, of YHWH in action, embodied in a human form. He would bring about the final redemption of God's people and thereby set in motion the fulfillment of Israel's destiny to be the light of the whole world.

This great theme comes into prominence in the last great journey of Jesus to Jerusalem. I argued two chapters ago that his action in the Temple constituted a decisive symbol of his messianic claim, his belief that it was his destiny to sum up Israel's long story in himself. I have suggested above that this action itself belonged to his belief that he was called to replace the Temple with his own presence and activity. I also argued that the great symbolic meal in the upper room was designed to symbolize his belief that through his death the redemption of Israel and thereby of the world would be accomplished. I now propose that these two actions were in fact the climactic symbolic moments, both of course pointing on to the cross and resurrection as their fulfillment, of a larger and yet more significant symbolic action. Jesus' last great journey to Jerusalem was intended, I suggest, to symbolize and embody the long-awaited return of YHWH to Zion. This journey, climaxing in his actions in the Temple and the upper room, and undertaken in full recognition of the likely consequences, was intended to function like Ezekiel lying on his side or Jeremiah smashing his pot. The prophet's action *embodied* the reality. Jesus was not content to *announce* that YHWH was returning to Zion. He intended to enact, symbolize and personify that climactic event. And he believed and said in appropriately coded language that he would be vindicated, would share the throne of Israel's God.

I cannot spell out the case for this view in any detail.[16] Suffice it to say that I have become convinced, the more I have studied them, that the stories Jesus told about a king or a master returning to see how his subjects or servants have been getting on with their tasks were never intended originally in the way so many Christian commentators have taken them, as predictions of the *second* coming of Jesus, with the

church as the subjects or servants awaiting his return and anticipating
some kind of judgment. The argument for this rereading of the parables in question is too detailed to reproduce here and must be studied
in that detail before one jumps to conclusions, but one or two points
may be made that should at least clear a path for the idea to make its
way into the surprised minds of those who meet it here for the first
time.

First, let me say as clearly as I can (since I have often been misunderstood at this point): I do not see this rereading of the parables of
the returning king/master as constituting a denial of the "second
coming" of Jesus.[17] Far from it. The belief that the creator God will at
the last recreate the whole cosmos and that Jesus will be at the center
of that new world is firmly and deeply rooted in the New Testament,
not least in such vital passages as Romans 8, 1 Corinthians 15 and
Revelation 21—22. But I do not think that Jesus talked about this
further event as such (except insofar as he spoke occasionally in
general terms about that complete redemption that we, with hindsight, know to be still in the future). Even granted that Jesus' hearers
did not always grasp what he said, it strains probability a long way
to think of him attempting to explain to people who had not grasped
the fact of his imminent death that there would follow an indetermi-
nate period after which he would "return" in some spectacular fashion, for which nothing in their tradition had prepared them.

In particular, I do not think these parables—I am thinking especially of Matthew 25:14-30 and its parallel in Luke 19:11-27, that is, the
parable(s) of the king/master giving his servants tasks and then
returning to assess their performance—teach this important truth. I
believe they were originally designed by Jesus to say something even
more important and (in his situation) more urgent: that, as he was
coming to Jerusalem for the last time, so YHWH was at last doing what
he had promised, returning to Zion to judge and to save. The thrust
of the parable is then to pick up Malachi's warning: "The Lord whom

you seek shall suddenly come to his Temple; but who may abide the day of his coming?" (3:1-2).

We can be quite clear that Luke at least understood the parable in this way.[18] His whole scene (it is always worth looking at the larger canvas on which Luke, ever the artist, paints his pictures) is designed to lead the eye up to the figure of Jesus, riding into Jerusalem on a donkey, sobbing his heart out as the crowds chant psalms of praise. And the words of warning he then speaks are words making it clear that, as far as Luke is concerned, this scene simply *is* the return of YHWH to Zion: your enemies, says Jesus, will leave not one stone upon another in Jerusalem, "because you did not know the time of your visitation." "Your visitation": a technical term for the coming of YHWH himself, not merely to "pay a visit" to his people in a casual way, but to "visit" them, in the older and more troubling sense, that is, to return to settle accounts with them, to bring all things to their appointed conclusion. The parable and the others like it were warning Israel that the moment had come; YHWH was indeed returning at last; but that this "coming" would mean not simply rescue and blessing for Israel but terrible judgment for those who had refused "the things that make for peace" (Lk 19:42).

All this enables us at least to grapple with and perhaps to understand some of the very cryptic things that Jesus is credited with saying in the last few days of his life. Having been quizzed by the scribes, Pharisees and Sadducees on various topics, Jesus poses them a riddle of his own: How can the scribes say that the Messiah is David's son?[19] According to Psalm 110, the Messiah is to share YHWH's throne, sitting at his right hand. Jesus seems to envisage, as the fulfillment of the messianic vocation that has embraced and taken him on this last journey to Jerusalem, that he will be enthroned at YHWH's right hand. This meaning must then be carried over into the trial scene, where in Mark 14:62 and parallels Jesus predicts that Caiaphas and his colleagues will see him vindicated, "sitting at the right hand of Power," that is, of God, as in Psalm 110, and "coming on the clouds of heaven" as in Daniel 7. The court will see Jesus vindicated and enthroned.

We must beware of misunderstanding what the Daniel passage means in this context. As we saw in chapter two, in Daniel 7 itself the "coming" of the Son of Man is an "upward" movement, not a "downward" one. There is no reason whatever to suppose that in Mark 14 or elsewhere in the Gospels this has been turned upside down (just as there is no reason to suppose that making this point constitutes a denial of the "second coming" of Jesus, merely a denial that this passage teaches that truth). Jesus is not predicting that he will literally, one day, fly downward on a literal cloud from the sky to the earth. So, too, it would be wrong to suppose that Jesus was telling Caiaphas and his colleagues that they would one day see him sitting on a physical throne. What they would see would be events heavy with meaning, with God-meaning, with Temple-meaning, with Jesus-meaning: the this-worldly events, from the rise of the post-Easter church to the fall of Jerusalem, which would indicate beyond any doubt that Israel's God had exalted Jesus, had vindicated him after his suffering and had raised him to share his own throne. The resurrection of Jesus, and all that followed from it, would be the evidence that Jesus was in the right all along.

This, I suggest, is the real reason for the charge of blasphemy at Jesus' trial. Confessing to being Messiah was not blasphemous (it might be foolish, it might be personally or politically dangerous, but it was not in itself an affront to YHWH). Threatening the Temple might come a bit closer—it was, after all, supposed to be YHWH's house— but there is no reason to suppose that making such a threat constituted actual blasphemy. What Jesus had done, I suggest, which made Caiaphas tear his robe and precipitated the court into its verdict (and the cunning transmuting of that theological verdict into a political one that Pilate would have to take notice of), was that, by way of answer both to the question about his Temple-action and to the question about his putative messiahship, he had quoted side by side the very two texts that, as we know from within the Jewish world of the day, could be used to indicate the enthronement, alongside YHWH himself, of the agent through whom the redemption would be accomplished.[20]

All of which brings us back full circle to where we began. Jesus' actions during the last week of his life focused on the Temple. Judaism had two great incarnational symbols: Temple and Torah. Jesus seems to have believed it was his vocation to upstage the one and outflank the other. Judaism spoke of the presence of her God in her midst, in the pillar of cloud and fire, in the Presence ("Shekinah") in the Temple. Jesus acted and spoke as if he thought he were a one-man counter-Temple movement. Judaism believed that her God would triumph over the powers of evil within Israel as well as outside. Jesus spoke of his own coming vindication, after his meeting the Beast in mortal combat. Jesus, too, used the language of the Father sending the Son. The so-called parable of the Wicked Tenants could just as well be the parable of the Son Sent at Last. His awareness, in faith, of the one he called Abba, Father, sustained him in his messianic vocation to Israel and to act as his Father's personal agent to her. So we could go on. Approach the incarnation from this angle and it is no category mistake but the appropriate climax of creation and covenant. Wisdom, God's blueprint for humans, at last herself becomes human. The Shekinah glory turns out to have a human face. "The Word became flesh," said John, "and tabernacled in our midst" (Jn 1:14; the Greek *eskēnosen*, often translated simply "dwelt," comes from the root *skēnē*, "tent" or "tabernacle"). John's theology, focused again and again on the Temple and on the way in which Jesus fulfilled its destiny, is after all rooted in the history that we have constructed from Matthew, Mark and Luke.

Conclusion

It is time to draw together the threads of this argument, and I can do no better than repeat what I have written elsewhere:

> I have argued that Jesus' underlying aim was based on his faith-aware-
> ness of vocation. He believed himself called, by Israel's god, to *evoke* the
> traditions which promised YHWH's return to Zion, and the . . . tradi-
> tions which spoke of a human figure sharing the divine throne; to *enact*
> those traditions in his own journey to Jerusalem, his messianic act in
> the Temple, and his death at the hands of the pagans (in the hope of
> subsequent vindication); and thereby to *embody* YHWH's return.[21]

There is no space to develop the point, but I believe that from here
we could in principle work our way through John's Gospel and
discover a fresh reading of many of its central passages.

What am I therefore saying about the earthly Jesus? In Jesus himself, I suggest, we see the biblical portrait of YHWH come to life: the
loving God, rolling up his sleeves (Is 52:10) to do in person the job that
no one else could do; the creator God, giving new life; the God who
works *through* his created world and supremely through his human
creatures; the faithful God, dwelling in the midst of his people; the
stern and tender God, relentlessly opposed to all that destroys or
distorts the good creation and especially human beings, but recklessly
loving all those in need and distress. "He shall feed his flock like a
shepherd; he shall carry the lambs in his arms; and gently lead those
that are with young" (Is 40:11). It is the Old Testament portrait of
YHWH, but it fits Jesus like a glove.

Let me be clear, also, what I am *not* saying. I do not think Jesus
"knew he was God" in the same sense that one knows one is hungry
or thirsty, tall or short. It was not a mathematical knowledge, like
knowing that two and two make four; nor was it straightforwardly
observational knowledge, like knowing that there is a bird on the
fence outside my room because I can see and hear it. It was more like
the knowledge that I have that I am loved by my family and closest
friends; like the knowledge that I have that sunrise over the sea is
awesome and beautiful; like the knowledge of the musician not only

of what the composer intended but of how precisely to perform the piece in exactly that way—a knowledge most securely possessed, of course, when the performer is also the composer. It was, in short, the knowledge that characterizes *vocation*. As I have put it elsewhere: "As part of his human vocation, grasped in faith, sustained in prayer, tested in confrontation, agonized over in further prayer and doubt, and implemented in action, he believed he had to do and be, for Israel and the world, that which according to Scripture only YHWH himself could do and be."[22]

Speaking of Jesus' "vocation" brings us to quite a different place from some traditional statements of gospel christology. "Awareness of vocation" is by no means the same thing as Jesus having the sort of "supernatural" awareness of himself, of Israel's God, and of the relation between the two of them such as is often envisaged by those who, concerned to maintain a "high" christology, place it within an eighteenth-century context of implicit Deism where one can maintain Jesus' "divinity" only by holding some form of docetism. This is the category, I suggest, enabling us finally to bring together the thoroughgoing historical study of Jesus within his first-century context and the rich awareness, so often ruled out in the name of "history," that Jesus believed it was his vocation to be the embodiment of that which was spoken of in the Jewish symbols of Temple, Torah, Word, Spirit and Wisdom, namely, YHWH's saving presence in the world, or more fully, in Israel and for the world. He believed it was his task to accomplish that which only YHWH could achieve: the great new exodus, through which the name and character of YHWH would be fully and finally unveiled, made known.

Or to quote once more from my fuller statement of this position:

> The return of YHWH to Zion, and the Temple-theology which it brings into focus, are the deepest keys and clues to gospel christology. Forget the "titles" of Jesus, at least for a moment; forget the attempts of some well-meaning Christians to make Jesus of Nazareth conscious of being

the second person of the Trinity; forget the arid reductionism that some earnest liberal theologians have produced by way of reaction. Focus, instead, on a young Jewish prophet telling a story about YHWH returning to Zion as judge and redeemer, and then embodying it by riding into the city in tears, symbolizing the Temple's destruction and celebrating the final exodus. I propose, as a matter of history, that Jesus of Nazareth was conscious of a vocation: a vocation, given him by the one he knew as "father," to enact in himself what, in Israel's scriptures, God had promised to accomplish all by himself. He would be the pillar of cloud and fire for the people of the new exodus. He would embody in himself the returning and redeeming action of the covenant God.[23]

All this leads in conclusion to the area that, it seems to me, is just as vital a part of the contemporary christological task as learning to speak truly about the earthly Jesus and his sense of vocation. We must learn to speak biblically, in the light of this Jesus, about the identity of the one true God.[24] There can be no more central task within our learning to follow Jesus and to transform our world with his gospel.

I return to what I said at the start. Western orthodoxy, not least within what calls itself "evangelicalism," has had for too long an overly lofty and detached view of God. It has always tended to approach the christological question by assuming this view of God and then by fitting Jesus into it. Hardly surprisingly, the result has been a docetic Jesus. This in turn generated the protest of the eighteenth century ("Jesus can't have been like that, therefore the whole thing is based on a mistake") and of much subsequent historical scholarship, not least because of the social and cultural arrangements that the combination of semi-Deism and docetism generated and sustained. That combination remains powerful, not least in parts of my own church, and it still needs a powerful challenge. My proposal is not that we know what the word *god* means and manage somehow to fit Jesus into that. Instead, I suggest that we think historically about a young Jew possessed of a desperately risky, indeed apparently crazy, vocation, riding into Jerusalem in tears, denouncing the Temple and dying on a Roman cross—and that we somehow allow our meaning for the word *god* to be recentered around that point.

Let me recapitulate and develop something I said in the opening chapter of this book. After twenty years of serious historical-Jesus study I still say the Christian creeds *ex animo,* but I now mean something very different by them, not least by the word *God* itself. The portrait has been redrawn. At its heart, as disclosed in the biblical writings, we discover a human face surrounded by a crown of thorns. God's purpose for Israel has been completed. Salvation is of the Jews, and from the King of the Jews it has come. God's covenant faithfulness has been revealed in the good news of Jesus, bringing salvation for the whole cosmos.

The thing about painting portraits of God is, of course, that, if they do their job properly, they should become icons. That is, they should invite not just cool appraisal—though the mind must be involved as well as the heart and soul and strength in our response to this God—but worship. That is fair enough, and I believe that this God is worthy of the fullest and richest worship that we can offer. But as with some icons, not least the famous Rublev painting of the three men visiting Abraham, the focal point of the painting is not at the back of the painting but on the viewer. Once we have glimpsed the true portrait of God, the onus is on us to reflect it: to reflect it as a community, to reflect it as individuals. Once we see who Jesus is, we are not only summoned to follow him in worship, love and adoration, but to shape our world by reflecting his glory into it.

The mission of the church, in fact, to which we shall turn in the final two chapters of this book, can be summed up in the phrase "reflected glory." It is precisely through engaging in the christological task, focusing on Jesus and allowing our picture of God to be shaped thereby not as a detached intellectual exercise but as the very heart of our worship, our praying, our thinking, our preaching and our living, that we are enabled to reflect that glory. When we see, as Paul says, the glory of God in the face of Jesus Christ, and when we rediscover the length and breadth of what that phrase means, we see and discover this not for our own benefit but so that the glory may shine in us and through us, to bring light and life to the world that still waits in darkness and the shadow of death.

CHAPTER SIX

THE CHALLENGE
OF EASTER

T*HE QUESTION OF JESUS' RESURRECTION LIES AT THE HEART OF THE* Christian faith. There is no form of early Christianity known to us—though there are some that have been invented by ingenious scholars—that does not affirm at its heart that after Jesus' shameful death God raised him to life again. Already by the time of Paul, our earliest written witness, the resurrection of Jesus is not just a single, detached article of faith. It is woven into the very structure of Christian life and thought, informing (among other things) baptism, justification, ethics and the future hope both for humans and for the cosmos.

In particular, the resurrection is the answer given by all of early Christianity to the fourth question about Jesus that we listed at the beginning. As well as Jesus' relation to Judaism, his aims and the reason for his death, the historian of the first century, no matter what his or her background may be, must inevitably ask: why did Christianity arise, and why did it take the shape it did? The early Christians themselves reply: we exist because of Jesus' resurrection. It is therefore incumbent upon the historian to investigate what precisely they meant by this and what can be said by way of historical comment upon this central and all-important belief.

I stress the historical angle from the outset because it has of course been argued, indeed insisted upon, in many circles that whatever we mean by the resurrection of Jesus, it is not accessible to historical investigation. As Dominic Crossan remarked about the study of Jesus in general, there have been some who said it could not be done, some who said it should not be done and some who said the former when they meant the latter.[1] Getting to the heart of these objections and answering them in detail would take us far too far afield within a single chapter. I simply wish to assert that the historian, so far from being debarred from the investigation of Jesus' resurrection, is in fact obligated to undertake such an investigation. Without it a large hole remains in the center of first-century history, no matter what presuppositions the historian may possess.

There have, of course, been several false trails in the investigation of this question, not least at a popular or semipopular level.

Barbara Thiering proposed that Jesus and the others crucified with him did not die, despite the two others having their legs broken, that one of them was actually Simon Magus, who was a doctor and had some medicine with him, which he gave to Jesus in the tomb so that he revived and was able to resume his career, traveling around with Paul and the others, not to mention getting married and having children.[2] This is simply a new and highly imaginative twist on an old hypothesis, that Jesus did not really die on the cross. As has been shown often enough, the Romans knew how to kill people, and the reappearance of a battered and exhausted Jesus would hardly be likely to suggest to his followers something for which they were certainly not prepared, namely, that he had gone through death and out the other side.

Equally, there are plenty of people who produce theories to explain that Jesus did not really rise from the dead, leaving an empty tomb behind him.

At a popular level, the BBC made a program in the mid-1990s built around the discovery in Jerusalem of an ossuary with the name "Jesus son of Joseph" on it. In the same tomb there were also ossuaries of people named Joseph, Mary, another Mary, a Matthew, and somebody called Judah, described as "son of Jesus." Not surprisingly, among the people who were unimpressed were the Israeli archaeologists, who knew that these names were exceedingly common in the first century. It was rather like finding John and Sally Smith in the London telephone directory.

A book was published in summer 1996 in which two intrepid researchers put together a fast-moving blockbuster of detective research involving the medieval Knights Templar, the Rosicrucians, the Freemasons, the Gnostics, concealed patterns in medieval paintings and so on, all to reach the conclusion that the bones of Jesus are now buried in a hillside in southwestern France, that the real message of the gospel was about living a good life and earning a spiritual, not bodily, resurrection and that the early church made up the doctrine of bodily resurrection as a way to gain political and financial power. The book is called *The Tomb of God*—ironically, because if Jesus' bones are in a tomb in France, there is no reason to suppose that he was or is God. And if they think belief in the resurrection was a way to power or money, they should read the New Testament and think again.

At least these ventures into popular-level pseudohistoriography reveal one thing: the question of Jesus' resurrection remains perennially fascinating, which is good news in an oblique sort of way. But they also reveal the amount of misinformation that swirls around the topic. One review of *The Tomb of God* began by telling its readers that the Christian belief in Jesus' resurrection meant that Jesus, after his death, was exalted to heaven. However, since traditionally Christians have believed that when they die their souls "go to heaven," leaving their bodies in the tomb, this is a highly misleading way of putting it. It makes it sound as though what happened to Jesus is simply what will happen, according to this belief, to all Christians as soon as they die, which is certainly not what the first Christians thought. That does not stop many people, at a popular level, from assuming that "Jesus rose from the dead" is simply a fancy way of saying "Jesus went to heaven when he died."

At the more serious scholarly level there has of course been plenty of continuing discussion of the resurrection. This has tended to take place, however, at the level of philosophical or systematic theological treatments. Those New Testament scholars who have written about the resurrection in recent times have tended to belong to the German tradition-historical school, who have attempted to probe back behind the details of the Gospel texts and of 1 Corinthians 15 to see where such traditions could have come from. But these, particularly the first two, have tended to be atomistic, to break the tradition down into its earliest hypothetical fragments; like much tradition-historical research they end with as many puzzles as they had at the start. What we have lacked has been a serious historical treatment of the subject from a writer firmly anchored within the history of Judaism of the first century.

The closest we have come to that have been hints in two writers who do not themselves appear to believe in the bodily resurrection of Jesus but who nevertheless say that something very strange really does seem to have happened. Geza Vermes, in his first book on Jesus, asserts that the tomb really must have been empty, and he does not seem to think that the disciples stole the body.[3] One of the greatest contemporary American writers about Jesus, Ed Sanders, speaks of Jesus' disciples as carrying on the logic of Jesus' own work "in a transformed situation," and says that the result of Jesus' life and work culminated in "the resurrection and the foundation of a movement which endured."[4] He forswears any special explanation or rationalization of the experiences of the disciples after Jesus' death. But he points out that on the one hand Jesus' disciples must have been prepared for a dramatic event that would establish the kingdom but that on the other hand what actually happened, which Sanders describes simply as "the death and resurrection," "required them to adjust their expectation, but did not create a new one out of nothing." Both Vermes and Sanders thus bear witness as historians of first-century Judaism to the great difficulty faced by any attempt to say that on the one hand nothing happened to the body of Jesus but that on the other hand Christianity began very soon after his death and began as precisely a resurrection-movement.

A serious problem that needs addressing before we begin our own argument is that the resurrection has from fairly early on in the church been regarded as the proof of Jesus' divinity. Resurrection and incarnation have thus been bound up together. This, indeed, is a possible reason why people have denied that the historian can pronounce on the resurrection, since the historian *qua* historian can hardly be expected to arrive at confident conclusions about God. But again this betrays a lack of historical thought. The Maccabean martyrs expected to be raised from the dead, but they certainly did not think this would make them divine. Paul argues that all Christians will be raised as Jesus was raised, but he does not suppose that they will thereby share the unique divine sonship that, in the same letter, he attributes to Jesus. Already in Paul, in fact, we see the clear distinction between "resurrection"—a newly embodied life after death—and "exaltation" or "enthronement," a distinction that some scholars have suggested only enters the tradition with Luke. But this is to run ahead of ourselves. For the moment we may simply note that whatever we think about Jesus' divinity, that cannot be the first meaning of his resurrection. The converse is also important. For the disciples to become convinced on other grounds that Jesus was divine would not of itself have led them to say that he had been raised from the dead.

Let me then propose a historical argument, focused mainly on the rise of the early church within the world of first-century Judaism, as to what must have happened on Easter morning or thereabouts. This is to treat the resurrection of Jesus as first and foremost a historical problem. There are three stages to this argument, each one of which contains the same four basic steps.[5]

The Rise of Early Christianity

As a kingdom-of-God movement. The first stage of the argument concerns the rise of Christianity within the Jewish world of its day as a kingdom-of-God movement. The four steps may be summarized as follows. First, early Christianity grew up as a kingdom-of-God movement; but second, "kingdom of God" in Judaism had certain particular meanings; third, since these certainly had not come to pass, we must enquire why the early Christians said that the kingdom of God had in fact been brought to birth; fourth, we must as historians postulate a reason for their strange affirmation. We must now spell out each of these steps a bit further.

First, early Christianity thought of itself as a kingdom-of-God movement. Already by the time of Paul the phrase "kingdom of God" had become more or less a shorthand for the movement, its way of life and its *raison-d'être*. And despite the attempts of some to suggest that this kingdom of God meant for the early Christians a new personal or spiritual experience rather than a Jewish-style movement designed to establish the rule of God in the world, all the actual evidence we have, as opposed to the fanciful would-be evidence that some have dreamed up on the basis of a hypothetical early Q and early *Thomas*, indicates that if Jesus' movement was a counter-Temple movement, early Christianity was a counter-empire movement. When Paul said "Jesus is Lord," it is clear that he meant that Caesar was not. This is not gnostic escapism but Jewish-style no-king-but-God theology with Jesus in the middle of it. And this theology generated and sustained not a group of gnostic-style conventicles but a Jewish-style new-covenant community.

Christianity was indeed, in the Jewish sense, a kingdom-of-God movement.

Second, however, within Judaism the coming kingdom of God meant, as we saw in earlier chapters, the end of Israel's exile, the overthrow of the pagan empire and the exaltation of Israel, and the return of YHWH to Zion to judge and save. Looking wider it meant the renewal of the world, the establishment of God's justice for the cosmos. It was not about a private existentialist or gnostic experience but about public events. If you had said to some first-century Jews "the kingdom of God is here" and had explained yourself by speaking of a new spiritual experience, a new sense of forgiveness, an exciting reordering of your private religious interiority, they might well have said that they were glad you had had this experience, but why did you refer to it as the *kingdom of God?*

Third, however, it was abundantly clear that the kingdom of God had not come in the way that first-century Jews had been imagining. Israel was not liberated; the Temple was not rebuilt; looking wider, it was obvious that evil, injustice, pain and death were still on the rampage. The question presses, then: Why did the early Christians say that the kingdom of God *had* come? One answer could obviously be: because they changed the meaning of the phrase radically so that it referred not to a political state of affairs but to an internal or spiritual one. But as we have seen, this is simply untrue to early Christianity. In the first written exposition of Christian kingdom-theology, which significantly enough is the same chapter as the first written exposition of the resurrection (1 Cor 15), Paul explained that the kingdom was coming in a two-stage process, so that the Jewish hope—for God to be all in all—would be realized fully in the future, following its decisive inauguration in the events concerning Jesus. The early Christians, in fact, not only used the phrase—used it so regularly, indeed, that when the early Gnostics wanted to produce their own new religion they borrowed the phrase even though it did not mean anything like what they were offering—but they reordered their symbolic world, their story-telling world, their habitual praxis, around it. They acted, in other words, as if the Jewish-style kingdom of God was really present. They organized their life as if they really were the returned-from-exile people, the people of the new covenant. At the same time we must ask: Why, in this process, did they *not* continue the sort of kingdom-revolution they had imagined Jesus was going to lead? How do we explain the fact that early Christianity was neither a nationalist Jewish movement nor an existential private experience?

Fourth, therefore, we must as historians postulate a reason to account for this group of first-century Jews who had cherished these kingdom-expectations, saying that their expectations had in fact been fulfilled, though not in the way they had imagined. The early Christians themselves with one voice say that the reason was the bodily resurrection of Jesus.

But before exploring this further we must move to the second stage of the argument. Christianity was not just a kingdom-of-God movement; it was, from the first, a *resurrection* movement. But what did resurrection mean to a Jew of the first century?

As a resurrection movement. As I have already remarked, there is no evidence for a form of early Christianity in which the resurrection was not a central belief. Nor was this belief, as it were, bolted on to Christianity at the edge. It was the central driving force, informing the whole movement.

But—the second step of the second stage of the argument—resurrection in first-century Judaism had a quite definite meaning. This is somewhat complex and controversial, and we need to spell it out a bit more fully.[6]

First, there was a spectrum of views in first-century Judaism concerning what happened to people after their death. There are some writings that speak of an ultimate nonphysical bliss; Philo and the

book of Jubilees are examples. There are some writings that insist that
the physical bodies of at least the righteous dead will be restored so
that (for instance) the martyrs will be, as one might say, put back
together again to confront their torturers and executioners and celebrate their downfall. The most obvious example of this is 2 Maccabees.
There are some writings that speak of a temporary disembodied state,
followed by a reembodiment. It is important to stress that Wisdom of
Solomon 2—3 belongs in this category and not in the same one as
Jubilees and Philo, despite the popular and indeed scholarly asser-
tions to the contrary effect. When Wisdom speaks of "the souls of the
righteous" as being "in the hand of God," this is emphatically not their
last resting place but a temporary safe haven before the time when
they will "shine forth and run like sparks through the stubble" and be
set by the Lord to rule over nations and kingdoms (3:1-8). This seems
to be the position of Josephus, at least when he is taking care to
describe what his fellow Jews actually believed as opposed to putting
speeches into the mouths of his heroes that he hopes will appeal to his
educated Roman audience. Finally, there are those who deny that
there is any continued existence after death: the Sadducees, notoriously, took this position, though they seem to have left no writings for
us to check up on them so that all we have are reports from people
who disagreed with them.

Within this spectrum two points need to be made very clearly. First,
though there was a range of belief about life after death, *the word*
resurrection *was only used to describe reembodiment, not the state of
disembodied bliss. Resurrection* was not a general word for "life after
death" or for "going to be with God" in some general sense. It was the
word for what happened when God created newly embodied human
beings after whatever intermediate state there might be.

Second, when people envisaged the state of temporary disembodiment prior to eventual resurrection, there was a variety of language
that they could use for it. They could be described as souls, or as angels

or some near equivalent, or as spirits, but not as resurrected bodies.

Resurrection meant reembodiment, but that was not all. From the time of Ezekiel 37 onward "resurrection" was an image used to denote the great return from exile, the renewal of the covenant, and to connote the belief that when this happened it would mean that Israel's sin and death (i.e., exile) had been dealt with, that YHWH had renewed his covenant with his people. Thus the resurrection of the dead became both metaphor and metonymy, both a symbol for the coming of the new age and itself, taken literally, one central element in the package. When YHWH restored the fortunes of his people then of course Abraham, Isaac and Jacob, together with all God's people down to and including the martyrs who had died in the cause of the kingdom, would be reembodied, raised to new life in God's new world. Where second-Temple Jews believed in resurrection, then, that belief had to do with the reembodiment of formerly dead human beings on the one hand and with the inauguration of the new age, the new covenant, in which all the righteous dead would be raised simultaneously on the other. That is presumably why, when Jesus spoke of the Son of Man rising from the dead as an individual within the continuing flow of history (Mk 9:10), the disciples were puzzled as to what he could be talking about.

Thus, if a first-century Jew said that someone had been "raised from the dead," the one thing they did not mean was that such a person had gone to a state of disembodied bliss, there either to rest forever or to wait until the great day of reembodiment. This can be tested by asking whether someone in 150 B.C. who believed passionately that the Maccabean martyrs were true and righteous Israelites, or someone in A.D. 150 who believed that Simeon ben-Kosiba was the true Messiah (if any such existed), would have said that they, or he, had been raised from the dead, intending by that statement to indicate simply that their cause was indeed righteous and that they were alive in a place of honor in the presence of God. The answer is obvious.

Someone in the position we have described might well have said that the martyrs, or ben-Kosiba, were alive in the form of either an angel or a spirit, or that their souls were in the hand of God. But they would not have dreamed of saying that they had already been raised from the dead. Resurrection meant embodiment and implied that the new age had dawned.

If, therefore, you had said to a first-century Jew "the resurrection has occurred," you would have received the puzzled response that it obviously had not, since the patriarchs, prophets and martyrs were not walking around alive again and since the restoration spoken of by Ezekiel 37 had clearly not occurred either. And if by way of explanation you had said that you did not mean that—that you meant, rather, that you had had a wonderful new sense of divine healing and forgiveness or that you believed the former leader of your movement was alive in the presence of God following his shameful torture and death—your interlocutor might have congratulated you on having such an experience and discussed with you such a belief. But he or she would still have been puzzled as to why you would use the phrase "the resurrection of the dead" to describe either of these things. That simply was not what the words meant.

But—this is the third step in this stage of the argument—as we have stressed before, the new age had not dawned in the way that first-century Jews imagined. Nor had the resurrection of all God's people of old taken place (though Matthew implies, in a very strange passage, that something like a foretaste of this happened after the crucifixion).[7] And yet the very earliest church declared roundly not only that Jesus was raised from the dead but that "the resurrection of the dead" had already occurred (Acts 4:2). What is more, they busily set about redesigning their whole worldview—their characteristic praxis, their controlling stories, their symbolic universe and their basic theology—around this new fixed point. They behaved, in other words, as though the new age had already arrived. That was the inner logic of the

Gentile mission, that since God had now done for Israel what he was going to do for Israel, the Gentiles would at last share the blessing. They did not behave as though they had had a new sort of religious experience or as if their former leader was (as the followers of the Maccabean martyrs would no doubt have said of their heroes) alive and well in the presence of God, whether as an angel or a spirit. The only explanation for their behavior, their stories, their symbols and their theology is that they really believed Jesus had been reembodied, had been bodily raised from the dead. This conclusion, in fact, is not often disputed today even among those who insist that the body of Jesus did in fact decompose in the tomb.

The fourth step in this second phase of the argument is, of course, to question whether the early church was right. We must postulate something that will account for this group of first-century Jews, including a well-educated Pharisee like Paul, coming so swiftly and so strongly to the conclusion that, against their expectations of *all* the righteous dead being raised to life at the *end* of the present age, *one person* had been raised to life in the *middle* of the present age. We shall look at the various possibilities presently.

As a messianic movement. I have already spoken about the way in which Christianity emerged as a messianic movement with the puzzling difference that, unlike all messianic movements known to us, its Messiah was someone who had already faced the Roman procurator—and had been executed by the Roman troops. I argued in chapter four that we cannot explain the rise of messianic beliefs by the resurrection alone; we must postulate, and the Gospels encourage us to accept, that Jesus acted and spoke messianically during his lifetime and that these actions and words were the proximate cause of his death. But equally we cannot explain why the early church continued to believe that Jesus was the Messiah if he had simply been executed by the Romans in the manner of failed Messiahs.

This is clear from the second step in the argument. Jewish expectations of a Messiah, as we have seen often enough, focused on defeating the pagans, rebuilding the Temple and bringing God's justice to the world. If a would-be Messiah was killed by the pagans, especially if he had not rebuilt the Temple, liberated Israel or brought justice to the world, that would be the surest sign that he was another in the long line of false Messiahs. The crucifixion of a Messiah did not say to a first-century Jew that he was the true Messiah and that the kingdom had come. It said exactly the opposite. It said that he was not and that it had not.

On the contrary. If the Messiah you had been following was killed by the pagans, you were faced with a choice. You could either give up the revolution, the dream of liberation—some went that route, notably, of course, the rabbinic movement as a whole after A.D. 135—or you could find yourself a new messiah, if possible from the same family as the late lamented one. Some went that route: witness the continuing movement that ran from Judas the Galilean in A.D. 6 to his sons or grandsons in the 50s, to another descendant, Menahem, during the war of 66-70, and to another descendent, Eleazar, who was the leader of the ill-fated Sicarii on Masada in 73. They worked that dynasty for all it was worth even though it kept coming to nothing. And once again let us be clear. If after the death of Simon bar-Giora in Titus's triumph in Rome you had suggested that Simon really was the Messiah, you would have invited a fairly sharp response from the average first-century Jew. If by way of explanation you said that you had had a strong sense of Simon still being with you, still supporting and leading you, the kindest response you might expect would be that their angel or spirit was still communicating with you—not that he had been raised from the dead.

So—the third step in the argument, once again—granting that Jesus of Nazareth was certainly crucified as a rebel king, being scourged as was Simon bar-Giora before execution, we are bound to regard it as extremely strange that the early Christians not only insisted that he was actually the Messiah, but reordered their worldview, their praxis, stories, symbols and theology around this belief. They had the two normal options open to them. They could have given up messianism as did the post-A.D. 135 rabbis and gone in for some form of private religion instead, whether of intensified Torah-observance or something else. They clearly did not do that; anything less like a private religion than going around the pagan world saying that Jesus was the *kyrios kosmou*, the Lord of the world, it would be hard to imagine. Equally and most interestingly they could have found themselves a new Messiah from among Jesus' blood-relatives. We know from various sources that Jesus' relatives continued to be important and well-known within the early church; one of them, James the brother of Jesus, though not having been part of the movement during Jesus' lifetime, became its central figure, the anchorman in Jerusalem while Peter and Paul went off around the world. Yet—and this is a vital clue, like Sherlock Holmes's dog that did not bark in the night—*nobody in early Christianity ever dreamed of saying that James was the Messiah.* Nothing would have been more natural, especially on the analogy of the family of Judas the Galilean. Yet James was simply known, even to Josephus in *Antiquities* 20, as "the brother of the so-called Messiah."

We are therefore forced once again—the fourth step in the third stage of the argument—to postulate something that will explain why this group of first-century Jews, who had cherished messianic hopes and focused them on Jesus of Nazareth, not only continued to believe that he was the Messiah after his death but actively announced him as such in the Jewish as well as the pagan world, cheerfully redrawing the picture of messiahship around him but refusing to abandon it.

Conclusion. Drawing this account of early Christianity within its Jewish context to a conclusion, we may observe the following points of continuity and discontinuity. The language of resurrection only makes sense within its first-century Jewish context, and it is clearly the presupposition for all early Christianity. However, the resurrection of one person, within the ongoing course of present history, was not what first-century Jews expected, and all the accounts we have of the risen Jesus describe the appearances in a way that indicates that there was a clear and well-known distinction to be drawn between those appearances and the experienced presence of Jesus with his church in the succeeding days and years. We are therefore forced, as a matter of history, to attempt to explain how it was that the early church came to make a claim that only made sense in the Jewish world, yet was not precisely what they as Jews had expected; how they came to describe Jesus in a certain way as the basis of their life and work, yet not in the way he was made known to them in their own day-to-day experience. That is the historical problem of the resurrection of Jesus. And to begin to answer the question, we must turn to our earliest written source: in this case, Paul.

Paul: 1 Corinthians 15

At this point some will no doubt say, following various popular writers: surely Paul, the first writer to mention the resurrection, refers simply to a spiritual body? Does this not mean that for him the resurrection was a nonphysical event? And, in any case, is not his "seeing" of Christ on the road to Damascus a pretty clear case of a "vision," to be explained in terms of his religious experience? Should we not suppose that all other "seeings" of Jesus were really like that, until the much later Gospel tradition came upon them and muddied the water by having Jesus cooking breakfast on the shore and even eating broiled fish?

We may note, as the beginning of an answer, that Paul is of course the classic example of the early Christian who has woven resurrection so thoroughly into his thinking and practice that if you take it away the whole thing unravels in your hands. We may note further that Paul of all people came from a Pharisaic background in which, as one of the strictest sort of Pharisees, he believed passionately in the restoration of Israel and the coming of the new age in which God would judge the world and rescue his people. This is the man we are reading when we turn to 1 Corinthians 15.

We may begin with verse 8. "Last of all, as to one untimely born, he appeared also to me." This is a violent image, invoking the idea of a Caesarian section, in which a baby is ripped from the womb, born before it was ready, blinking in shock at the sudden light, scarcely able to breathe in this new world. We detect here not simply a touch of autobiography as Paul reflects on what it had felt like on the Damascus Road. We trace a clear sense that Paul knew that what had happened to him was precisely *not* like what had happened to the others. What is more, he only just got in as a witness to the resurrection before the appearances stopped; when he says "last of all," he means that what one might call the ordinary Christian experience of knowing the risen Jesus within the life of the church, of prayer and faith and the sacraments, was not the same sort of thing that had happened to him. He distinguishes his Damascus Road experience, in other words, both from all previous seeings of the risen Jesus and from the subsequent experience of the church, himself included.

Moving back to the start of the chapter, then, we find in verses 1-7 what Paul describes as the very early tradition that was common to all Christians. He received it and handed it on; these are technical terms for the handing on of tradition, and we must assume that this represents what was believed in the very earliest days of the church back in the early 30s. The tradition includes the burial of Jesus (conveniently ignored by Crossan, who suggests darkly that Jesus' body was eaten by dogs as it hung on the cross so that there was nothing left to bury).[8] In Paul's world, as has been said often enough but still not heard by all scholars, to say that someone had been buried and then raised three days later was to say that the tomb was empty— though the emptiness of the tomb, so important in twentieth-century discussion, was clearly not something that Paul felt the need to stress.

For him, saying "resurrection" was quite enough to imply that and much more. There is simply no evidence to suggest that the word could mean to a well-taught Jew halfway through the first century that the person concerned was alive and well in a nonphysical sphere while his body was still in a tomb.

Paul does not, in the list of appearances, mention the appearances to the women. This is not (as is sometimes suggested) because he or the framers of the tradition were chauvinistic, but because this common tradition was designed for use in preaching, where the people listed were clearly regarded as witnesses to the resurrection. In that culture, of course, women were not regarded as reliable witnesses. His mention of the five hundred who saw Jesus at one time cannot be assimilated to the Pentecost-experience mentioned in Acts 2, as some have tried to do, because it precedes the appearance to James, and James was already on board with the early movement by the time of Pentecost.

But perhaps the most important thing about the first paragraph of 1 Corinthians 15 is what Paul understood the resurrection to *mean*. For him it was not a matter of the opening up of a new religious experience. Nor was it a proof of survival, of life after death. It meant that the Scriptures had been fulfilled, that the kingdom of God had arrived, that the new age had broken in to the midst of the present age, had dawned upon a surprised and unready world. It all happened "according to the Scriptures"; which, as I have argued elsewhere, does not mean that Paul could find a few biblical proof-texts for it if he hunted hard enough but that the entire biblical narrative had at last reached its climax, had come true in these astonishing events.[9] As a result, Paul can then, in the course of verses 12-28, argue that the coming of the new age is a two-stage affair: the Messiah first, then finally the resurrection of all those who belong to the Messiah. We should note most carefully, in view of our earlier discussion, that the Messiah is not envisaged as being in the present time a soul, a spirit or an angel. He is not in an intermediate state, awaiting a time when he will finally be raised from the dead. He is *already* risen; he is already, as a human being, exalted into the presence of God; he is already ruling the world, not simply in some divine capacity but precisely as a human being, fulfilling the destiny marked out for the human race from the sixth day of creation.[10]

On this basis Paul can move in verses 29-34 to assert most emphatically the future embodiedness both of the Christian dead and of the Christian living, or to put it somewhat more precisely, the future *re*embodiment of the Christian dead and the future *transformed* embodiment of the Christian living. This, he says, is the only explanation within the Jewish worldview, where alone this language makes any sense, for the present practice of the church, both in terms of the strange practice of baptism for the dead and in the more accessible image of his apostolic labors (v. 34, looking on to v. 58). The present life of the church, in other words, is not about "soul-making," the attempt to produce or train disembodied beings for a future disembodied life. It is about working with fully human beings who will be reembodied at the last, after the model of the Messiah.

But what sort of a body will this be? We may jump ahead for a moment to verses 50-57. There Paul states clearly and emphatically his belief in a body that is to be *changed,* not abandoned. The present physicality in all its transience, its decay and its subjection to weakness, sickness and death, is not to go on and on forever; that is what he means by saying "flesh and blood cannot inherit the kingdom of God." For Paul "flesh and blood" does not mean "physicality" *per se* but the corruptible and decaying present state of our physicality. What is required is what we might call a "noncorruptible physicality": the dead will be raised "incorruptible" (v. 52), and we—that is, those who are left alive until the great day—will be changed. As in 2 Corinthians 5 Paul envisages the present physical body "putting on" the new body as a new mode of physicality over and above what we presently know.

This is not mere resuscitation, but equally it is emphatically not disembodiment. And if this is what Paul believes about the resurrection body of Christians, we may assume (since his argument works from the one to the other) that this was his view of the resurrection of Jesus as well.

In between the passages we have just briefly examined comes the most complex part of the chapter, verses 35-49. There Paul speaks of the different kinds of physicality, between which there exist both continuity and discontinuity. Within this, when he speaks of the future resurrection body as a "spiritual body," he does *not* mean, as has often been suggested, a "nonphysical" body. To say that is to allow into the argument a Hellenistic worldview that is quite out of place in this most Jewish of chapters. He is contrasting the present body, which is a *sōma psychikon*, with the future body, which is a *sōma pneumatikon*. *Sōma* means "body," but what do the two adjectives mean? Here the translations are often quite unhelpful, particularly RSV and NRSV with their misleading rendering of "physical body" and "spiritual body." Since *psychē*, from which *psychikon* is derived, is regularly translated "soul," we might as well have assumed that Paul thought that the present body too was nonphysical! Since that is clearly out of the question, we are right to take both phrases to refer to an actual physical body, animated by "soul" on the one hand and "spirit"—clearly God's spirit—on the other. (We may compare Romans 8:10f., where God's Spirit is the agent in the resurrection of Christians.) The present body, Paul is saying, is "a [physical] body animated by 'soul' "; the future body is "a [transformed physical] body animated by God's Spirit."

One final note about Paul's view of resurrection. It is often said, as we noted earlier, that he and indeed many other early Christians did not distinguish between resurrection and exaltation and that, if anything, exaltation was the primary category for them, with the resurrection of the body being a later development. First Corinthians 15 clearly gives the lie to this. The exaltation of Jesus is clearly distinguished from the resurrection. Of course, since the risen Jesus is the same person as the exalted Lord and since his resurrection is the prior condition for his exaltation, there is close continuity between the two. Where his argument requires it (as, for instance, in Phil 2:5-11), Paul is quite capable of referring only to the exaltation, not to the resurrection. But in this passage where he sets the matter out more fully than anywhere else, the two are aligned without confusion and distinguished without dislocation.

Paul, then, writing in the early 50s and claiming to represent what the whole main stream of the church believed, insisted on certain things about the resurrection of Jesus.

1. It was the moment when the creator God fulfilled his ancient promises to Israel, saving them from "their sins," i.e., from their exile. It thus initiated the "last days," at the end of which the victory over death begun at Easter would at last be complete.

2. It involved the transformation of Jesus' body: it was, that is to say, neither a resuscitation of Jesus' dead body to the same sort of life nor an abandonment of that body to decomposition. Paul's account presupposes the empty tomb.

3. It involved Jesus' being seen alive in a very limited early period, after which he was known as present to the church in a different way. These early sightings constituted those who witnessed them as apostles.[11]

4. It was the prototype for the resurrection of all God's people at the end of the last days.

5. It was thus the ground not only for the future hope of Christians but for their present work.

Conclusion: The Gospel Traditions and the Resurrection

I have concentrated on the large-scale historical argument and on the earliest written document, namely, 1 Corinthians. But as we turn our gaze wider toward the rest of the New Testament and early Christianity I suggest that we find Paul's perspective reaffirmed at every turn. The resurrection narratives of the Gospels, for all their puzzling nature and apparent conflicts, are quite clear on three points.

First, the sightings of and meetings with Jesus are quite unlike the sort of heavenly visions or visions of a figure in blinding light or dazzling glory or wreathed in clouds that one might expect in the Jewish apocalyptic or mystical traditions. They are not, that is to say, attempting to describe the sort of thing one would expect if what he or she wanted to say was simply that Jesus had been exalted to a position of either divinity or at least heavenly glory. The portrait of Jesus himself in these stories does not appear to have been modeled on existing stories of "supernatural appearances." It was not created out of expectation alone.

Second, the body of Jesus seems to be both physical, in the sense that it was not a nonmaterial angel or spirit, and transphysical, in the sense that it could come and go through locked doors. As I read the Gospel accounts, I have a sense that they are saying, in effect, "I know this is extraordinary, but this is just how it was." They are, in effect, describing more or less exactly that for which Paul provides the underlying theoretical framework: an event for which there was no precedent and of which there remains as yet no subsequent example, an event involving neither the resuscitation nor the abandonment of a physical body, but its transformation into a new mode of physicality.

Third, the accounts are quite clear that the appearances of Jesus were not the sort of thing that went on happening during the continuing existence of the early church. Luke did not suppose that his readers might meet Jesus on the road to Emmaus. Matthew did not expect his audience to meet him on a mountain. John did not suppose that people were still liable to come upon Jesus cooking breakfast by the shore. Mark certainly did not expect his readers to "say nothing to anyone, for they were afraid."

From this point of view I find it totally incredible to suppose (as a good many New Testament scholars have done) that the Gospel accounts of the resurrection, especially Luke and John, represent a late development in the tradition, in which for the first time people thought it appropriate or even necessary to speak of Jesus in such an overtly physical fashion. The idea that traditions developed from a more Hellenistic early period to a more Jewish later period is in any case extremely odd and though widely held this century ought to be abandoned as unwarranted and in any case counterintuitive. I suggest that whenever the Gospels of John and Luke reached their final form, the traditions embodied now in their closing chapters go back to genuine early memories, told and retold no doubt, shaped and reshaped by the life of the community that retold them but with their basic message preserved intact. It was not the sort of thing, quite frankly, that people in that world spoke or wrote about. All attempts to show that the resurrection narratives in the Gospels are derived from other literature have conspicuously failed.

Without going into more details, for which there is no space here, let me mention very briefly the added strengths that this view can claim. It is often pointed out that the tomb of Jesus was not venerated in the manner of the tombs of the martyrs. It is often noted that we have to explain in very early Christianity the emphasis on the first day of the week as the Lord's Day. It is not so often pointed out that the burial of Jesus was intended as the first part of a two-stage burial; had his body been still in a tomb somewhere, someone would sooner or later have had to collect the bones and put them in an ossuary, and the game would have been up. These and similar considerations force the eye back to the first Easter day and to the question we have asked all along: what precisely happened?

Among those who deny the bodily resurrection of Jesus, one theory is particularly common at the present time. Some have argued that Peter and Paul experienced some sort of visionary hallucination.

Peter, they say, was overcome with grief and perhaps guilt and experienced what people in that state often do: a sense of the presence of the lost person with him, talking to him, reassuring him. Paul, they say, was in a state of fanatical guilt, and this induced a similar fantasy in him. The two of them then communicated their experience enthusiastically to the other disciples who underwent a kind of corporate version of the same fantasy.

This theory is not new, though it has been revived in new ways. It is a kind of updated version of a mainline Bultmannian theory according to which, though the body of Jesus remained in the tomb, the disciples came into a new experience of the love and grace of God; or the view of Schillebeeckx, that when the disciples went to the tomb, their minds were so filled with light that it did not matter whether there was a body there or not. I have no time to discuss these theories in detail. But I have to say that as a historian I find them far harder to accept than the stories told by the evangelists themselves, for all their problems.

For a start, if Peter or Paul had had such experiences, the category that would have suggested itself would not be "resurrection"; it would be that of the appearance of Jesus' "angel" or his "spirit."[12] If one had described such an experience to a first-century Jew, and even if such a person had been enthused to the extent of experiencing something similar himself or herself, it would never have convinced them that the age to come had burst into the present time, that it was now time for the Gentiles to hear the good news, that the kingdom was really here, that Jesus was after all the Messiah. I believe, therefore, that the only way forward for us as historians is to grasp the nettle, recognizing that we are of course here at the borders of language, of philosophy, of history and of theology. We had better learn to take seriously the witness of the entire early church, that Jesus of Nazareth was raised bodily to a new sort of life, three days after his execution.

And it is this, of course, that offers far and away the best explanation of the rise of that same early church. All other explanations leave far more questions unsolved than solved. In particular, it explains why the church came so very early to believe that the new age had dawned; why, in consequence, they came to believe that Jesus' death had not been a messy accident, the end of a beautiful dream, but rather the climactic saving act of the God of Israel, the one God of all the earth; and why, in consequence, they, to their own astonishment, arrived at the conclusion that Jesus of Nazareth had done what, according to the Scriptures, only Israel's God could do. In that sense the resurrection pointed them toward that full christology that they came to hold within twenty or so years. But the critical thing right from the beginning was that the resurrection of Jesus demonstrated that he was indeed the Messiah, that Jesus had indeed borne the destiny of Israel on his shoulders in carrying the Roman cross outside the city walls, that he had gone through the climax of Israel's exile and had returned from that exile three days later according to and in fulfillment of the entire biblical narrative, and that his followers in being the witnesses to these things were thereby and thereupon commissioned to take the news of his victory to the ends of the earth. If the study of Jesus in his historical context is to be more than a mere exercise in ancient history, albeit an utterly fascinating one, it is perhaps at this point that we can observe the way in which it points beyond itself. The line that begins with the historical Jesus moves forward into the historical present, offering as much of a challenge to the world of late-twentieth-century postmodernity as it did to the world of second-Temple Judaism and the early Roman empire. But for that we shall need another chapter—or, to be more precise, another two.

CHAPTER SEVEN

WALKING TO EMMAUS IN A POSTMODERN WORLD

W*E NOW COME TO THE POINT WHERE, AFTER A GOOD DEAL OF* historical reconstruction, the reader may well be asking the question that has exercised this author too over many years: So what? How do we move from the detailed, historical reconstruction of this Jesus, living in the world of the first century, to our own world with all its very different contours and agendas?

The last place we reached in our historical inquiry was Jesus' resurrection, and it is there that I begin in these two last chapters. In the present chapter I shall bring together one of the best-known stories of Jesus' resurrection, namely, Luke's description of the two disciples on the road to Emmaus, and a brief consideration of the postmodern world in which we find ourselves. I want to let them knock some sparks off each other, producing, I hope, illumination in both directions. And to help them do this, I want to set the discussion in the context of one of the most moving and poignant poems in the Old Testament, namely, the combined psalm we know as Psalms 42 and 43.

Mission in a Postmodern World?

Let me spell out first the context within which we find ourselves in the Western world today.[1] We live at the overlap of several huge cultural waves. At the social and economic level we moved two or three hundred years ago from an agricultural economy to an industrial one, and a great many implicit values and aspirations within our culture changed drastically as a result. Many still cherish a yearning to be rooted in agriculture and feel frustrated as that becomes increasingly impossible. But we are now moving rapidly away from the modernist industrial economy and into a world where the microchip carries more muscle and generates more money than the factory chimney. Politicians and industrialists alike are caught up in the clash between the two quite different cultures. Patterns of work, economic growth, social and cultural values are being turned inside out in the process.

This quite sudden and threatening transition is bound up with the great move that has come about in recent years from what has been called modernity to what has been called postmodernity. To oversimplify, this has focused on three areas.

Knowledge and truth. Where modernity thought it could know things objectively about the world, postmodernity has reminded us that there is no such thing as neutral knowledge. Everybody has a point of view, and that point of view distorts; everybody describes things the way that suits them. There is no such thing as objective truth. Likewise, there are no such things as objective values, only preferences. The cultural symbols that encapsulate this revolution are the personal stereo and the virtual-reality system: everyone creates his or her own private world.

The self. Modernity vaunted the great lonely individual, the all-powerful "I": Descartes' *cogito ergo sum* and the proud "I am the master of my fate, the captain of my soul." But postmodernity has deconstructed the self, the I. The "I" is just a floating signifier, a temporary and accidental collocation of conflicting forces and impulses. Just as reality collapses inward upon the knower, the knower him- or herself deconstructs.

The story. Modernity told an implicit narrative about the way the world was. It was essentially an eschatological story. World history had been steadily moving toward or at least eagerly awaiting the point where the industrial revolution and the philosophical Enlightenment would burst upon the world, bringing a new era of blessing for all. This huge overarching story—overarching stories are known in this world as metanarratives—has now been conclusively shown to be an oppressive, imperialist and self-serving story; it has brought untold misery to millions in the industrialized West and to billions in the rest of the world, where cheap labor and raw materials have been ruthlessly exploited. It is a story that serves the interests of the Western world. Modernity stands condemned of building a new tower of Babel. Postmodernity has claimed, primarily with this great metanarrative as the example, that *all* metanarratives are suspect; they are all power games.

Collapsing reality; deconstructing selfhood; the death of the metanarrative. These are the keys to understanding postmodernity. It is a ruthless application of the hermeneutic of suspicion to everything that the post-Enlightenment Western world has held dear. It goes exactly with the microchip revolution, which has generated and sustained a world in which creating new apparent realities, living in one's own private world and telling one's own story even though it does not cohere with anybody else's, is easier and easier. This is what the Internet is partly all about. We live in a cultural, economic, moral and even religious hypermarket. Scoop up what you like and mix it all together.

What does the church do when faced with this huge swirling set of cultural movements and tensions?

Most of us who are now adult Christians learned our trade, learned

Christianity, learned to preach and live the gospel, within the resolutely modernist and industrial world. Some branches of Christianity, it is true, have managed to hold on to a premodern way of thinking and even of living, holding the modern world, let alone the postmodern world, at arm's length. But most of us who have been practicing Christians for half a century or so have traditionally articulated the gospel to people who thought and felt as modern people, particularly as progress people: people who thought that if they worked a little harder and pulled their weight a bit more strongly, everything would pan out. That modernist dream, translated into theology, sustains a sort of Pelagianism: pull yourself up by your moral bootstraps, save yourself by your own efforts. And since that was what Martin Luther attacked with his doctrine of justification by faith, we have preached a message of grace and faith to a world of eager Pelagians. And we have announced a pure spiritual message, uncorrupted by political and social reflection.

That looks fine to begin with. If you meet a Pelagian coming down the street, give him or her Augustine or Luther. But there are at least two problems with it. First, it is not actually what Paul himself meant by justification by faith. That is another subject for another day.[2] But second, with the move to postmodernity, most of our contemporaries already, and all of them soon, will not be Pelagians any longer. Those who have abandoned the smokestack economy for the microchip, those who have denied all objective knowledge in favor of a world of feelings and impulses, those who have abandoned the arrogant Enlightenment "I" for the deconstructed mass of signifiers, those who have torn down the great metanarrative and now play with different interchangeable stories as they come along—those who live in this world, which is increasingly our world, are not trying to pull themselves up by their moral bootstraps. Where would they pull themselves up to? Why would they bother? Who are "they," anyway? Motive, goal, identity—all these have been undermined by the shifting sands of postmodernity.

Faced with this, many Christians have tried—some are still trying—to deny the presence of postmodernity, to retain the modern world that we felt so comfortable in, to which we preached a modernist gospel (whether we realized it or not). Many want to turn the clock back, culturally and theologically. It cannot be done. My proposal in these last two chapters is that we should not be frightened of the postmodern critique. It had to come; it is, I believe, a necessary judgment on the arrogance of modernity, a judgment from within. Our task is to reflect on that moment and, reflecting biblically and Christianly, to see our way through the moment of despair and out the other side. That is why I want to discuss further the resurrection and the Emmaus Road story, and to do so through the lens of the poem we call Psalms 42 and 43.

Psalms 42 and 43

The psalms we call 42 and 43 are in fact a single poem, in three stanzas. Each stanza ends with some version of the great refrain:

> Why are you cast down, O my soul,
>   and why are you disquieted within me?
> Hope in God; for I shall again praise him,
>   my help and my God.

And this psalm contains the great prayer, which we do well to echo as we consider our own calling: "O send out your light and your truth; let them lead me; let them bring me to your holy hill, and to your dwelling. Then I will go to the altar of God, to God my exceeding joy; and I will praise you with the harp, O God, my God" (Ps 43:3-4).

Let us look quickly through the poem so that we see its shape and thrust. The whole piece is about being in the presence of God. At its most obvious level the poem is by someone who has experienced the presence of God in the Temple in Jerusalem; he remembers the excitement of being close to God, and it creates a deep ache and sense of loss because he is not there any more.

So in verses 1-5 he is in a state of (what we would call) deep depression:

> As a deer longs for flowing streams,
>   so my soul longs for you, O God.
> My soul thirsts for God, for the living God.
>   When shall I come and behold the face of God?
> My tears have been my food day and night,
>   while people say to me continually, "Where is your God?"
> These things I remember, as I pour out my soul:
>   how I went with the throng,
>   and led them in procession to the house of God,
> with glad shouts and songs of thanksgiving,
>   a multitude keeping festival.
> Why are you cast down, O my soul,
>   and why are you disquieted within me?
> Hope in God; for I shall again praise him,
>   my help and my God.

He is thirsty for God, like a deer in the desert; he finds himself in tears twenty-four hours a day; his memory of happier times only makes him feel worse. All he can do is engage in an inner dialogue: *Why are you so heavy? Hope in God—I shall again worship him.*

Then, in 42:6-11, he remembers what it was like being in the presence of God:

> My soul is cast down within me;
>   therefore I remember you from the land of Jordan and of Hermon,
>   from Mount Mizar.
> Deep calls to deep at the thunder of your cataracts;
> all your waves and your billows have gone over me.
> By day YHWH commands his steadfast love,
>   and at night his song is with me,
>   a prayer to the God of my life.
> I say to God, my rock, "Why have you forgotten me?

Why must I walk about mournfully because the enemy oppresses
me?"
As with a deadly wound in my body, my adversaries taunt me,
while they say to me continually, "Where is your God?"
Why are you cast down, O my soul,
and why are you disquieted within me?
Hope in God; for I shall again praise him,
my help and my God.

He is a long way away from Jerusalem—in the land of Jordan or up
on Mount Hermon. He knows that in theory YHWH is there with him,
and he can pray to him, but he feels a long way off. Enemies oppress
him, and people taunt him with the apparent lack of any evidence for
the presence of God. He longs to be back in Jerusalem, where he can
sense God's presence and grace, where everyone is caught up with
worship and adoration, and again he reminds himself simply to hope.
Telling yourself to hope is not the same as hoping; but if it is all you
can do, it is better than nothing.

Then in what we call Psalm 43, which is actually the third and last
stanza of the same poem, the problem comes more into focus. The
psalmist is not just geographically distant from the home of God; he
is surrounded by people whose whole way of life is radically opposed
to God:

Vindicate me, O God, and defend my cause against an ungodly people;
from those who are deceitful and unjust deliver me!
For you are the God in whom I take refuge; why have you cast me off?
Why must I walk about mournfully
because of the oppression of the enemy?
O send out your light and your truth, let them lead me;
let them bring me to your holy hill and to your dwelling.
Then I will go to the altar of God, to God my exceeding joy;
and I will praise you with the harp, O God, my God.
Why are you cast down, O my soul, and why are you disquieted within
me?
Hope in God; for I shall again praise him, my help and my God.

The enemies are ungodly, deceitful and unjust. He is powerless before them, and God seems to have abandoned him. It is at this point, the low point of the whole poem, that he prays the great prayer upon which the whole poem turns (43:3): the prayer for God's light and truth to come and find him, to lead him home, to bring him back to praise God once more. He is far away from Jerusalem and needs to be led back with joy, like Israel in the wilderness being led by the pillar of cloud and fire, the strange symbolic presence of the living God. Light and truth are what you need not just when your intellect is curious and needs stimulating but when your whole being is lost, downcast, depressed, thirsty for God. And then he returns once again to the refrain: "Why are you cast down? Hope in God; I shall again praise him, my help and my God."

Hold this poem in your mind as we turn to the New Testament and use the language and imagery it supplies as the visual backdrop or perhaps the musical accompaniment to the story we are now going to examine, the story of the two disciples on the road to Emmaus: Luke 24:13-35.

The Road to Emmaus

If Luke is an artist, this is one of his most sublime paintings:

> Now on that same day, two of them were going to a village called Emmaus, about seven miles from Jerusalem, and talking with each other about all these things that had happened. While they were talking and discussing, Jesus himself came near and went with them, but their eyes were kept from recognizing him. And he said to them, "What are you discussing with each other while you walk along?" They stood still, looking sad. Then one of them whose name was Cleopas, answered him, "Are you the only stranger in Jerusalem who does not know the things that have taken place there in these days?" He asked them, "What things?" They replied, "The things about Jesus of Nazareth, who was a prophet mighty in deed and word before God and all the people, and how our chief priests and leaders handed him over to be con-

demned to death and crucified him. But we had hoped that he was the one to redeem Israel. Yes, and besides all this, it is now the third day since these things took place. Moreover, some women of our group astounded us. They were at the tomb early this morning, and when they did not find his body there, they came back and told us that they had indeed seen a vision of angels who said that he was alive. Some of those who were with us went to the tomb and found it just as the women had said; but they did not see him." Then he said to them, "Oh, how foolish you are, and how slow of heart to believe all that the prophets have declared! Was it not necessary that the Messiah should suffer these things and then enter into his glory?" Then beginning with Moses and all the prophets, he interpreted to them the things about himself in all the scriptures.

As they came near the village to which they were going, he walked ahead as if he were going on. But they urged him strongly, saying, "Stay with us, because it is almost evening and the day is now nearly over." So he went in to stay with them. When he was at the table with them, he took bread, blessed and broke it, and gave it to them. Then their eyes were opened, and they recognized him; and he vanished from their sight. They said to each other, "Were not our hearts burning within us while he was talking to us on the road, while he was opening the scriptures to us?" That same hour they got up and returned to Jerusalem; and they found the eleven and their companions gathered together. They were saying, "The Lord has risen indeed, and he has appeared to Simon!" Then they told what had happened on the road, and how he had been made known to them in the breaking of the bread.

We must first consider what was going on within the events Luke here describes.

It is the afternoon of the first Easter day. All sorts of strange things have happened in the morning, and the disciples still do not have a clue what has been going on. As the day wears on, two of them set off to go home to Emmaus. They are joined by a mysterious stranger, who engages them in conversation about the new events. If we are to understand this section historically, it is vital that we grasp the central point, stated in verse 21. "We were hoping," say the two of them, "that he was the one who would redeem Israel."

Where were they coming from? What was their problem?

They had been living out of a story, a controlling narrative. This story was built up from historical precedents, prophetic promises and of course from the songs of the psalter. The exodus was the backdrop. God's subsequent liberations of his people from various foreign powers formed successive narrative layers all pointing in the same direction. When pagan oppression was at its height, Israel's God would step in and deliver her once more. "Why are you so heavy, O my soul? Why so cast down within me? Hope in God—for I will yet praise him, my help and my God."

In particular, as we have already seen, most first-century Jews believed that the exile was not yet really over. The great prophetic promises had not been fulfilled. Israel still needed "redeeming"— which, in their language, was an obvious code for the exodus. The exodus was the great covenant moment; what they now needed was covenant renewal. So we may imagine them praying Psalm 43 in this very concrete situation: "Vindicate me, O God, defend my cause against the ungodly people! Deliver me from the deceitful and unjust! Send out your light and your truth; let them lead me! Why are you so heavy, O my soul; hope in God!" The Hebrew Scriptures thus offered to Jesus and his contemporaries *a story in search of an ending.* Jesus' followers had thought the ending was going to happen with Jesus. And it clearly had not.

How had they thought it would happen? The pattern of messianic and prophetic movements in the centuries either side of Jesus tells a fairly clear story. The method was quite simple: holiness, zeal for God and the law, and military revolt. The holy remnant with God on their side would defeat the pagan hordes. Thus it had always been in Scripture; thus, they believed, it would be when the great climax came, when Israel's God would become King of all the world. "We were hoping that he would be the one to redeem Israel." They were doing what the psalm told them to: "Hope in God; for I shall again praise him, my help and my God."

The crucifixion of Jesus was therefore the complete and final devastation of their hopes. Crucifixion is what happens to people who think they are going to liberate Israel and find out too late that they are mistaken. It is not simply that Jesus' followers knew from Deuteronomy that a crucified person was under God's curse. Nor was it simply that they had not yet worked out a theology of Jesus' atoning death. The crucifixion already had, for them, a thoroughly theological as well as political meaning: it meant that the exile was still continuing, that God had not yet forgiven Israel's sins, that the pagans were still ruling the world. Their thirst for redemption, for God's light and truth to come and lead them, was still not satisfied. All of this we must, as historians, hold in our minds if we wish to understand the most basic level of Luke 24.

This explains, of course, why the two disciples were arguing so vigorously. They had been traveling up a road they thought was leading to freedom, and it turned out to be a cul-de-sac. As they explain to the mysterious stranger, all the signs were right: Jesus of Nazareth had indeed been a prophet mighty in deed and word; God had been with him, and the people had approved him. Surely he was the one through whom the story would reach its climax, and Israel would be free! How could they possibly have been so mistaken—as his execution by their leaders and rulers showed they had been? And now confusion has become worse, confounded because of strange reports about a missing body and a vision of angels. This has nothing to do with what they have been hoping for. It is a disturbing extra puzzle on top of the deep sorrow and disappointment they are feeling. The two disciples in this story are not feeling guilty at having run away, as people so often say in describing Easter. They are feeling sad, let down, possibly even angry. "I say to God my rock, 'Why have you forgotten me? Why must I walk about mournfully because the enemy oppresses me?' "

The response from the stranger is *to tell the story differently* and to show that within the historical precedents, the prophetic promises and the psalmists' prayers there lay a constant theme and pattern to which they had hitherto been blind. Israel's sufferings increased in Egypt to the screaming point, and then the redemption occurred. Israel cried to the Lord in her suffering, and he raised up judges to deliver her. The Assyrians swept through the country and surrounded Jerusalem; they were routed by YHWH himself when they were on the point of taking the city. When Israel is cast down, walking about mournfully because of the oppression of the enemy, then her God will act, sending out his light and truth to lead her like the pillar of cloud and fire in the wilderness.

And though Babylon had succeeded where Assyria failed, to be followed by the other pagan nations climaxing now with Rome, the prophets pointed into the gloom and declared that it would be *through* this darkness that the redemption would come. Israel would be narrowed down to a point, a remnant, a Servant, one like a Son of Man attacked by monsters, and this little group would pass through the raging waters and not drown, through the fire and not be harmed. Somehow, strangely, the saving purposes of YHWH for Israel and through Israel for the world would be carried through the most intense suffering, to emerge the other side as exile was at last undone, as sins were at last forgiven as an act in history, as the covenant was renewed, as the kingdom of God was finally established.

This then, was after all how the story worked; this was the narrative the prophets had been elaborating. Yes, the Scriptures were indeed to be read as a narrative reaching its climax. They never were a mere collection of arbitrary or atomized proof-texts. But no, the story was never about Israel beating up her enemies and becoming established as the high-and-mighty masters of the world. It was always the story of how the creator God, Israel's covenant God, would bring his saving purposes for the world to birth through the suffering and vindication of Israel. "Beginning with Moses and all the prophets, he interpreted to them in all the Scriptures the things concerning himself." This could never be a matter of so-called "messianic" proof-texts alone. It was the entire narrative, the complete story-line, the whole world of prayer and hope, focused on Israel as the bearer of God's promises for the world, then focused on the remnant as the bearer of Israel's destiny, and focused finally on Israel's true king as the one upon whom the task even of the remnant would finally devolve. He had been the servant for the servant-people. He had done for Israel and the world what Israel and the world could not do for themselves.

Their slowness of heart and lack of belief in the prophets had not, therefore, been a purely spiritual blindness. It had been a matter of telling and living the wrong story. But now, suddenly, with the right story in their heads and hearts, a new possibility, huge, astonishing and breathtaking, started to emerge before them. Suppose the reason the key would not fit the lock was because they were trying the wrong door. Suppose Jesus' execution was not the clear disproof of his messianic vocation but its confirmation and climax. Suppose the cross was not one more example of the triumph of paganism over God's people but was actually God's means of defeating evil once and for all. Suppose this was, after all, how the exile was designed to end, how sins were to be forgiven, how the kingdom was to come. Suppose this was what God's light and truth looked like, coming unexpectedly to lead his people back into his presence.

As this strange realization began creeping over them, they arrived at their house and invited the stranger to stay with them. He quietly assumed the role of host, taking, blessing and breaking the bread. They recognized him, and he vanished. And with that recognition the story of the last hour itself suddenly made sense: "Did not our heart burn within us while he talked to us on the road, as he opened the Scriptures to us?" (v. 32). And their testimony to each other turned into eager testimony to the others as they hurried back to Jerusalem, where their own news was met with answering news from the eleven: The Lord has indeed risen—he has appeared to Simon! Then they told what had taken place on the road and how he was known to them in the breaking of the bread.

Notice what has happened. Their prayer has been answered. Their longing has been satisfied. They have returned to God's holy hill and to his dwelling. God's light and truth have led them back, and their sorrow has been turned into praise.

Already, of course, we are not just telling the bare facts of what happened. There are, after all, no such things as bare facts, least of all in a story like this. But we have been focusing on the disciples themselves. Let's shift the focus for a few moments, and look at what Luke is doing with the story.

Emmaus on Luke's Larger Canvas

The first thing to point out is Luke's stress on the surprising fulfillment of Scripture in the death and resurrection of Jesus. At the key moments in each section of the chapter—verses 7, 26f., 44f.—he underlines the fact that the story he has been telling makes sense and only makes sense as the great climax of the story told by Moses, the prophets and the psalms: that is, the story of how the creator God is saving the world through his people, Israel, with that action now visibly focused on Jesus, the Messiah. We content ourselves here with just one of these features.

The way in which Luke has told the central story of this chapter invites us to compare and contrast it with Genesis 3. The man and the woman are in the garden, beginning the task set before them of being God's image-bearers in his newly created world, that is, of bringing God's love and care and wise ordering to bear upon the whole creation. The woman took the forbidden fruit and gave it to the man, and they both ate it; "and the eyes of them both were opened, and they knew that they were naked" (Gen 3:7). And they began in sorrow and shame to argue about responsibility and to go out into a puzzling world of thorns and thistles.

Luke wants to tell us that this story has now been reversed. I take it that the couple on the road were husband and wife, Cleopas and Mary (cf. Jn 19:25). The thorns and thistles of their world have been puzzling enough, and they stand in sorrow and shame with their hopes in tatters. Following Jesus' astonishing exposition of Scripture, they come into the house; Jesus takes the bread, blesses it and breaks it, "and their eyes were opened, and they recognized him." (The Greek is very close to the Septuagint of Genesis 3:7.) They thereby become part of the vanguard for God's project of restoring the world in which his image-bearers take his forgiving love and wise ordering—that is, his kingdom—to the whole of creation. Earle Ellis points out in his commentary that the meal in Emmaus is the eighth meal-scene in the Gospel, where the Last Supper was the seventh: the week of the first creation is over, and Easter is the beginning of the new creation.[3] God's new world order has arrived. The exile is over—not just Israel's exile in actual and spiritual Babylon but the exile of the human race, shut out of the garden. The new world order does not look like people thought it would, but they must get used to the fact that it is here and that they are not only its beneficiaries but also its ambassadors and witnesses.

Within this new world there is a new awareness of who Jesus is. Consider how Luke has used this story as the balancing frame to the story he told way back at the beginning about the boy Jesus in the Temple (Lk 2:41-52). The whole village goes to Jerusalem for the Passover. When the feast is done, Jesus' parents set off for home with all the family and friends. Eventually they realize that Jesus is not with them. They panic. They rush back to Jerusalem and spend three days looking for him. Eventually they find him—in the Temple. "Didn't you know," he says, "that I would be about my Father's business?" And they did not understand what he meant.

Observe what Luke has done. Here is the later Passover. Here are the two going away from Jerusalem. They have waited for three days in agony of spirit, and now they are leaving the city. This time Jesus is with them but incognito. "Didn't you know," he says, "that this is how it had to be?" And now their eyes are opened, and they know him, and they rush back to Jerusalem full of joy.

In framing the rest of his Gospel in this way, Luke has given us a historical version of Psalms 42 and 43. Here in Luke 2 are Mary and Joseph, and here are the two on the road, thirsty for God and not finding him, living with sorrow and tears away from Jerusalem. Here is another couple in Luke 24 also sorrowful, and here is the light and truth of God in the person of Jesus, the exposition of Scripture and the breaking of bread, and they are led back to Jerusalem, back to God's city, back to the place of hope and promise. The last line of Luke's Gospel picks up Psalm 43:4: they worshiped him and returned to Jerusalem with great joy, and they were continually in the Temple, praising God. Somewhere along the road, literally and metaphorically, God's light and truth had come to lead them, to lead them into his very presence, to the place where hope gives way to joy and mourning to dancing.

And how has this come about? It has happened because the Messiah himself has gone to the place of pain, the place where Israel and indeed the whole world was in deep distress. He has been cast down, oppressed by the enemy. He quoted the threefold refrain of Psalm 42 and 43 in Gethsemane: "My soul is exceedingly sorrowful"; and, on the cross, he acted out Psalm 42:9: "I say to God, my rock, 'Why have you forgotten me?' " He became the suffering Israel on behalf of the suffering Israel; he went into exile—Israel's exile, the human exile from the garden, the exile of the whole cosmos—to redeem those who were in exile. And in so doing he became on the cross, in the resurrection, on Easter morning, the very embodiment of Psalm 43:3: this is what God's light and truth look like when at last in response to a thousand years of prayer they come forth from God's presence to lead God's people to his holy hill and to his dwelling, back from the place of tears to the place of hope and joy. Where are God's light and truth in this story? Are they not there, incognito, on the road, leading the disciples to understand the Scriptures, strangely known in the breaking of the bread? And does that not lead us to say that God's light and truth were there, like the pillar of cloud and fire on the previous Friday afternoon, in the wilderness of Calvary, outside the city walls, outside the garden, the place of tears, the place where God seems to have hidden his face forever?

The last point to make about the way that Luke has told the story concerns the central symbol, carefully repeated, at the heart of the Emmaus narrative. Jesus is recognized when he takes the bread, blesses it and breaks it (v. 30ff.). Yes, says Luke a few verses later, summing up the excited announcement of the two disciples: they described what had happened on the road—which we already know means the full-dress exposition of Scripture, the retelling of God's story—and how he had been made known to them *in the breaking of the bread*. Now, unless we are extremely deaf, we can hardly miss what Luke is saying. The last time Jesus had broken the bread was, of course, at the Last Supper (22:19). And the first Lukan summary of the whole life of the church is found in Acts 2:42 in these words: "They continued eagerly in the apostles' teaching, and in the common life, in the breaking of bread, and the prayers." The only reason for "breaking of bread" in such a list is if that *breaking* carried particular significance. Luke's first audience would have heard him bring together the exposition of Scripture and the breaking of bread, the word and the sacrament, the story and the symbol, as the central and normative marks of the church's life. The heart is warmed, says Luke, when Scripture is expounded so as to bring out the true story, and the Lord is known in the breaking of the bread. The two belong together, interpreting each other and together pointing to the new world, the new vocation, the kingdom of God and above all to Jesus himself as the climax of Israel's history and now the Lord of the world.

And in terms of Luke's rereading of the whole Old Testament story we discover at last how we might reread Psalms 42 and 43 within a specifically Christian setting. The Temple, the place where God has promised to dwell with his people, is quietly but decisively replaced— by Jesus himself. And the Temple worship is replaced by the breaking of bread in Jesus' name. Why are you cast down, O my soul? Why are you so disquieted within me? Hope in God—in the Word made flesh, in the God who wept in Gethsemane and who became God-forsaken on Calvary, in the God who comes to you incognito on the road, who comes as light and truth to lead you to his holy hill and to his dwelling, who prepares a table before you in the presence of your enemies, who makes himself known in the breaking of the bread. Hope in this God and you will again praise him, your help and your God.

From Emmaus to Dover Beach

What does all this have to say about Christian mission in a postmodern world? Let me recapitulate what I said at the beginning. We have had our noses rubbed in the fact that reality is not all it was cracked up to be; what we thought was hard fact turns out to be somebody's propaganda. We have been startled to discover that the autonomous self, so highly prized from the eighteenth to the twentieth century within the Western world, not least in some versions of Christianity, has been deconstructed into the turmoil of various forces and drives. We have watched as the postmodern world has torn down the controlling stories by which modernity, including Christian modernity, ordered its world. All we are left with is the great postmodern virtual smorgasbord where you can pick and choose what you want.

How are you to address this world with the gospel of Jesus? You cannot just hurl true doctrine at it. You will either crush people or drive them away. That is actually not a bad thing, because mission and evangelism were never actually meant to be a matter of throwing doctrine at people's heads. They work in a far more holistic way: by praxis, symbol and story as well as what we think of, in a somewhat modernist way, as "straightforward" exposition of "truth." I am reminded of St. Francis's instructions to his followers as he sent them out: preach the gospel by all means possible, he said, and if it's really necessary *you could even use words.* I am reminded, too, of the power of symbolic praxis to go beyond words when I think of one of the greatest ballerinas of all time. After one of her great performances somebody had the temerity to ask her what the dance *meant.* Her reply was simple and speaks volumes to us as we consider mission in the postmodern world. "If I could have said it," she said, "I wouldn't have needed to dance it."

I suggest, in fact, that if postmodernism functions as the death of modernist culture, many of us will find ourselves like the disciples on the road to Emmaus. We as Western Christians mostly bought a bit too heavily into modernism, and we are shocked to discover that it has been dying for a while and is now more or less completely dead. We need to learn how to listen for the hidden stranger on the road who will explain to us how it was that these things had to happen, and how there is a whole new world out there waiting to be born, for which we are called to be the midwives. The answer to the challenge of postmodernism is not to run back tearfully into the arms of modernism. It is to hear in postmodernity God's judgment on the follies and failings, the sheer selfish arrogance, of modernity and to look and pray and work for the resurrection into God's new world out beyond. We live at a great cultural turning point; Christian mission in the postmodern world must be the means of the church grasping the initiative and enabling our world to turn the corner in the right direction.

We must therefore get used to a mission that includes living the true Christian praxis. Christian praxis consists in the love of God in

Christ being poured out in us and through us. If this is truly happening, it is not damaged by the postmodern critique, the hermeneutic of suspicion. We must get used to telling the story of God, Israel, Jesus and the world as the true metanarrative, the story of healing and self-giving love. We must get used to living as those who have truly died and risen with Christ so that our self, having been thoroughly deconstructed, can be put back together, not by the agendas that the world presses upon us but by God's Spirit.

Those who find themselves caught up in the story, who learn to reorder their lives according to the symbols, are again and again summoned with a vocation. The vocation is part of the truth; and again and again we only understand God, insofar as we ever do, when the story, symbol and praxis come together in our own lives, when we in turn go through Psalms 42 and 43, from despair to worship, when we in turn walk sorrowfully on the road to Emmaus, only to find our hearts burning within us at the opening of Scripture, our eyes opened to the presence of God in Christ in the breaking of the bread and our feet suddenly energized to go and tell the good news to others.

My judgment, therefore, is that the present cultural crisis in the Western world is not to be wished away as a silly and transient phenomenon. Postmodernity may often be expressed in silly and ephemeral ways, but the basic critique of modernist arrogance, including Christian modernist arrogance, is right on target. What we must not do, I believe, is to pretend that it has not really happened, to cling to modernity in some shape or form because to admit that postmodernity has made its point is to connive with the forces of destruction. That would be like the two disciples trying to pretend that Jesus had not really been crucified, that he was still around somewhere, that everything was really all right, that those wicked, indeed diabolical, Roman soldiers had not really killed him. It might have been nice for them to hold on to their earlier dreams, but they would have been living a lie, not the truth. To admit that the soldiers

really did kill Jesus would not have been to connive with them, to sup
with the devil; it was simply to recognize the truth.

But nor can we construct a Christian worldview from within postmodernity itself. Our task is to discover, in practice, what the equivalent of the resurrection might be within our culture and for our times.
There is no way back to the easy certainties of modernism, whether
Catholic or Protestant, fundamentalist or liberal. The only way is
forward, forward into God's freshly storied world, forward with the
symbols that speak of death and resurrection, forward with the hum-
ble praxis of the gospel—and forward in that multilayered context
with fresh thoughts, fresh arguments, fresh intellectual understanding. Foolish ones, slow of heart to understand what God was up
to! Was it not necessary that modernist versions of Christianity should
die in order that truth might be freshly glimpsed, not as a set of
doctrines or theories but as a person and as persons indwelt by that
person?

And then how long must it be before we learn that our task as
Christians is to be in the front row of constructing the post-postmodern world? The individual existential *angst* of the sixties has become
the corporate and cultural *angst* of the nineties. The human beings
who could not pull themselves together in the 1960s have become the
human societies that cannot put themselves together in the 1990s.
What is the Christian answer to it all? The Christian answer to it is the
love of God, which goes through death and out the other side. What
is missing from the postmodern equation is of course love. The radical
hermeneutic of suspicion that characterizes all of postmodernity is
essentially nihilistic, denying the very possibility of creative or healing
love. In the cross and resurrection of Jesus we find the answer: the God
who made the world is revealed in terms of a self-giving love that no
hermeneutic of suspicion can ever touch, in a Self that found itself by
giving itself away, in a Story that was never manipulative but always
healing and recreating, and in a Reality that can truly be known,

indeed to know which is to discover a new dimension of knowledge, the dimension of loving and being loved.

We have a chance at the end of one millennium and the start of another to announce this message to the world that so badly needs it. I believe we have this as our vocation: to tell the story, to live by the symbols, to act out the praxis and to answer the questions in such a way as to become in ourselves and our mission in God's world the answer to the prayer that rises inarticulately, now, not just from one puzzled psalmist but from the whole human race and indeed the whole of God's creation: "O send out your light and your truth; let them lead me; let them bring me to your holy hill and to your dwelling." And when we ourselves are grasped by that light and that truth, by the strange glory of God in the face of Jesus Christ, we from within the crisis of truth in the contemporary world can say to those parts of our world that are still puzzled, to those parts of ourselves that are still dismayed: "Why are you cast down? Why so disquieted? Was it not necessary that these things should happen? Hope in God; for we shall again praise him, our help and our God." And we shall say it not just with words but with deeds: with policies, with symbolic praxis, that reveal in action the healing love of God.

Let me end with a parable, returning once more to the story of the Emmaus road. This parable functions against the background of one of the great symbols of modernist secularism, Matthew Arnold's poem "Dover Beach." There Arnold describes from his late-nineteenth-century perspective the way in which what he calls "the sea of faith" has emptied; the tide has gone out; all we can hear is the "melancholy, long, withdrawing roar" of the distant sea, leaving us in the gloom where, all too prophetically, "ignorant armies clash by night."

Two serious-minded unbelievers are walking home together, trying to make sense of the world of the mid-1990s. The dream of progress and enlightenment has run out of steam. Critical postmodernity has blown the whistle on the world as we knew it.

Our two unbelievers walk along the road to Dover Beach. They are discussing, animatedly, how these things can be. How can the stories by which so many have lived have let us down? How shall we replace our deeply ambiguous cultural symbols? What should we be doing in our world now that every dream of progress is stamped with the word *Babel*?

Into this conversation comes Jesus, incognito. (It is a good thing they don't recognize him because modernism taught them to disbelieve in all religions, and postmodernism rehabilitated so many that Jesus is just one guru among dozens.) "What are you talking about?" he asks. They stand there, looking sad. Then one of them says, "You must be about the only person in town who doesn't know what a traumatic time the twentieth century has been. Nietzsche, Freud and Marx were quite right. We had a war to end wars, and we've had nothing but more wars ever since. We had a sexual revolution, and now we have AIDS and more family-less people than ever before. We pursued wealth, but we had inexplicable recessions and ended up with half the world in crippling debt. We can do what we like, but we've all forgotten why we liked it. Our dreams have gone sour, and we don't even know who 'we' are anymore. And now even the church has let us down, corrupting its spiritual message with talk of cosmic and political liberation."

"Foolish ones," replies Jesus; "How slow of heart you are to believe all that the Creator God has said! Did you never hear that he created the world wisely? and that he has now acted within his world to create a truly human people? and that from within this people he came to live as a truly human person? and that in his own death he dealt with evil once and for all? and that he is even now at work, by his own Spirit, to create a new human family in which repentance and forgiveness of sins are the order of the day, and so to challenge and overturn the rule of war, sex, money and power?" And, beginning with Moses and all the prophets, and now also the apostles and prophets of the New Testament, he interprets to them in all the Scriptures the things concerning himself.

They arrive at Dover Beach. The sea of faith, having retreated with the outgoing tide of modernism, is full again, as the incoming tide of postmodernism proves the truth of Chesterton's dictum that when people stop believing in God they don't believe in nothing, they believe in *anything.* On the shore there stands a great hungry crowd who had cast their bread on the retreating waters of modernism only to discover that the incoming tide had brought them bricks and centipedes instead. The two travelers wearily begin to get out a small picnic basket, totally inadequate for the task. Jesus gently takes it from them, and within what seems like moments he has gone to and fro on the beach until everyone is fed. Then the eyes of them all are opened, and they realize who he is, and he vanishes from their sight. And the two say to each other, "Did not our hearts burn within us on the road, as he told us the story of the creator and his world, and his victory over evil?" And they rush back to tell their friends of what happened on the road and how he had been made known in the breaking of the bread.

Actually, that is not a story. It is a play, a real-life drama. And the part of Jesus is to be played by you and me. This is Christian mission in a postmodern world. And in case anyone wants things spelled out more specifically as to either the basis of this activity or what it means in practice, the last chapter of this book will attempt at least to point in the right direction.

CHAPTER EIGHT

THE LIGHT
OF THE WORLD

I WANT NOW TO DRAW TOGETHER THE THREADS OF ALL THAT HAS BEEN
dealt with so far and to shape and focus it a bit more specifically on
the task that faces Christians at the start of the third millennium. If we
believe in any sense that Jesus is the light of the world, how do we
move from looking at Jesus and seeing the challenge he posed to his
contemporaries, to shedding the light of this same Jesus on our own
world? How do we come to terms with the challenge that faces us,
that of relating the true Jesus to our own tasks, not least but not only
in the academic and professional spheres—and equally that of facing
today's world with the challenge of Jesus?

As we have seen, this bringing together of the historical study of
Jesus and the contemporary task of the church is often felt to be deeply
problematic. I have said previously and am sure many of my readers
have thought that when we put Jesus firmly and clearly into his own
first-century Jewish context, and see how his message related uniquely
and specifically to that situation, it seems much harder to get any sense
of his relevance for today. We are so used to reading (for instance) the
parables or the Sermon on the Mount as addressed basically to us, to

our churches, to Christians in general, and as inculcating a particular spirituality, teaching great timeless truths or pointing toward particular ethical norms, that we are frightened of allowing the basic meaning of the text to be something quite different, namely, Jesus' unique challenge to his contemporaries, leading to his unique death on the cross. I want in this final chapter to argue that this fear is groundless and that on the contrary we can move forward from the uniqueness of Jesus to a powerful, focused and deeply relevant way of following him and shaping our world with the message and work of his gospel.

To understand how you get from the unique, unrepeatable significance of Jesus' own mission and message to Israel to the calling of the church in our own day or any day, the first thing to do is to grasp the full significance of the bodily resurrection of which I wrote two chapters ago. We have far too often flattened out the resurrection into meaning simply that there is life after death after all; this is of course something that few ordinary Jews of Jesus' day would have denied. Or we have seen its significance simply in the fact that Jesus is alive today, and we can get to know him. That is gloriously true, but it is not the specific truth of Easter itself. The many-sided truth of Easter is set out in many passages in the New Testament but emerges particularly in John's Gospel. And in John 20:1, 19, John tells us quite plainly: Easter day is the first day of the week.

John doesn't waste words. When he tells us something like this twice, he knows what he's doing. It isn't just that Easter day happened to be on a Sunday. John wants his readers to figure out that Easter day is the first day of God's new creation. Easter morning was the birthday of God's new world. On the sixth day of the week, the Friday, God finished all his work; the great shout of *tetelestai*, "It is finished!" in John 19:30 looks all the way back to the sixth day in Genesis 1 when, with the creation of human beings in his own image, God finished the initial work of creation. Now, says John (19:5), "Behold the Man!" here on Good Friday is the truly human being. John then invites us to see the Saturday, the sabbath between Good Friday and Easter day in terms of the sabbath rest of God after creation was done:

> On the seventh day God rested
>   in the darkness of the tomb;
> Having finished on the sixth day
>   all his work of joy and doom.
> Now the word had fallen silent,
>   and the water had run dry,
> The bread had all been scattered,
>   and the light had left the sky.
> The flock had lost its shepherd,
>   and the seed was sadly sown,
> The courtiers had betrayed their king,
>   and nailed him to his throne.
> O Sabbath rest by Calvary,
>   O calm of tomb below,
> Where the grave-clothes and the spices
>   cradle him we did not know!
> Rest you well, beloved Jesus,
>   Caesar's Lord and Israel's King,
> In the brooding of the Spirit,
>   in the darkness of the spring.

Then on Easter morning it is the first day of the week. Creation is complete; new creation can now begin. The Spirit who brooded over the waters of creation at the beginning broods now over God's world, ready to bring it bursting to springtime life. Mary goes to the tomb while it's still dark and in the morning light meets Jesus in the garden. She thinks he is the gardener, as in one important sense he indeed is. This is the new creation. This is the new Genesis.

On the first day of the week, then, in the evening when the doors were shut for fear, Jesus came and stood in the midst and said, "Peace be with you." The being and knowing of the old world are no longer limitations. What was relevant in the old week is made redundant in the new. With the new creation, a new order of being has burst upon the startled old world, opening up new possibilities. And the message that accompanies this is the age-old Jewish message of Shalom, Peace: not just a standard greeting but deeply indicative again of the achievement of the cross, as John at once indicates: "Saying this, Jesus showed them his hands and his side."

With this comes (Jn 20:19-23) the commission, the word that stands at the head of all Christian witness, mission, all discipleship, all reshaping of our world. "Peace be with you," he said again; "as the Father sent me, so I send you." And he breathed on them as once, long ago, God had breathed into the nostrils of Adam and Eve his own breath, his breath of life. Receive the Holy Spirit. Forgive sins and they are forgiven; retain them and they are retained.

It is this three-sided commissioning that I want to explore now as we look at Jesus as the light of the world, the challenge that faces every generation. The three sides are these: (1) as the Father sent me, so I send you; (2) receive the Holy Spirit; (3) forgive sins and they are forgiven, retain them and they are retained. Let me back up for a moment and introduce these three from a wider angle than simply this narrative in John.

I said earlier that the whole New Testament assumes that Israel was chosen to be the people through whom the creator God would address and solve the problems of the whole world. Salvation is of the Jews. The early Christians believed that the one true God had been faithful to that promise and had brought salvation through the king of the Jews, Jesus himself. Israel was called to be the light of the world; Israel's history and vocation had devolved on to Jesus, solo. He was the true Israel, the true light of the whole world.

But what did it mean to be the light of the world? It meant, according to John, that Jesus would be lifted up to draw all people to himself. On the cross Jesus would reveal the true God in action as the lover and savior of the world. It was because Israel's history with God and God's history with Israel came to its climax in Jesus, and because

Jesus' story reached its climax on Calvary and with the empty tomb, that we can say: here is the light of the world. The Creator has done what he promised. From now on we are living in the new age, the already-begun new world. The light is now shining in the darkness, and the darkness has not overcome it.

This means that the church, the followers of Jesus Christ, live in the bright interval between Easter and the final great consummation. Let's make no mistake either way. The reason the early Christians were so joyful was because they knew themselves to be living not so much in the *last* days, though that was true too, as in the *first* days—the opening days of God's new creation. What Jesus did was not a mere example of something else, not a mere manifestation of some larger truth; it was itself the climactic event and fact of cosmic history. From then on everything is different. Do not put all the eschatological weight on that which is still to come. The whole point of New Testament Christianity is that the End came forward into the present in Jesus the Messiah.

But it would be equally mistaken to forget that after Easter, after Pentecost, after the fall of Jerusalem, the final great consummation is still to come. Paul speaks of this in Romans 8 and 1 Corinthians 15: the creation itself will receive its exodus, will be set free from its slavery to corruption, death itself will be defeated, and God will be all in all. Revelation 21 speaks of it in terms of new heavens and new earth.[1] In all of these scenarios the most glorious thing is of course the personal, royal, loving presence of Jesus himself. I still find among the most moving words I ever sing in church are those in the old Christmas carol "Once in Royal David's City":

> And our eyes at last shall see him,
> Through his own redeeming love.

Blessed, says Jesus, are those who have not seen yet believe; yes, indeed, but one day we shall see him as he is and share the completed new creation that he is even now in the process of planning and making. We live, therefore, between Easter and the consummation, following Jesus Christ in the power of the Spirit and commissioned to be for the world what he was for Israel, bringing God's redemptive reshaping to our world.

Let us be clear, too, about the relation between our present work, our present reshaping of our world and the future world that God intends to make. Christians have always found it difficult to understand and articulate this and have regularly distorted the picture in one direction or the other. Some have so emphasized the discontinuity between the present world and our work in it on the one hand and the future world that God will make on the other that they suppose God will simply throw the present world in the trash can and leave us in a totally different sphere altogether. There is then really no point in attempting to reshape the present world by the light of Jesus Christ. Armageddon is coming, so who cares about acid rain or third-world debt? That is the way of dualism; it is a radically anticreation viewpoint and hence is challenged head on by (among many other things) John's emphasis on Easter as the first day of the new week, the start of God's new creation.

On the other hand, some have so emphasized the continuity between the present world and the coming new world that they have imagined we can actually build the kingdom of God by our own hard work. I am thinking not just of the old so-called liberal social gospel but also of some aspects of the Calvinist heritage, which in its reaction against perceived dualisms of one sort or another has sometimes played down the radical discontinuity between this world and the next. This is sorely mistaken. When God does what God intends to do, this will be an act of fresh grace, of radical newness. At one level it will be quite unexpected, like a surprise party with guests we never thought we would meet and delicious food we never thought we would taste. But at the same time there will be a rightness about it, a rich continuity with what has gone before so that in the midst of our surprise and delight we will say, "Of course! This is how it had to be, even though we'd never imagined it."

The point of continuity that I want to emphasize here, because it is so central to our task of shaping God's world, our world, is found at the end of 1 Corinthians 15. The chapter, as we saw earlier, is a massive, detailed and complex account of the final resurrection and the nature of our future embodiment. Right at the end in verse 58 Paul says something that could seem like an anticlimax. You or I, writing a chapter on the resurrection, would probably finish with a shout of praise at the glorious future that awaits us. That would be appropriate too. But Paul finishes like this: "Therefore, my beloved family, be steadfast, immovable, always abounding in the work of the Lord, inasmuch as you know that in the Lord your labor is not in vain." What is he saying? Just this: that part of the point of bodily resurrection is that there is vital and important *continuity* as well as discontinuity between this world and that which is to be, precisely because the new world has already begun with Easter and Pentecost, and because everything done on the basis of Jesus' resurrection and in the power of the Spirit already belongs to that new world. It is already part of the kingdom-building that God is now setting forward in this new week of new creation.

That is why Paul speaks in 1 Corinthians 3:10-15 of Jesus as the foundation and of people building on that foundation with gold, silver or precious stones, or as it may be, with wood, hay and stubble. If you build on the foundation in the present time with gold, silver and precious stones, *your work will last.* In the Lord your labor is not in vain. You are not oiling the wheels of a machine that is soon going over a cliff. Nor, however, are you constructing the kingdom of God by your own efforts. You are following Jesus and shaping our world in the power of the Spirit; and when the final consummation comes, the work that you have done, whether in Bible study or biochemistry, whether in preaching or in pure mathematics, whether in digging ditches or in composing symphonies, will stand, will last.

The fact that we live within this eschatological framework, between, so to speak, the beginning of the End and the end of the End, should enable us to come to terms with our vocation to be for the world what Jesus was for Israel, and in the power of the Spirit to forgive and retain sins. The image that helps me as I wrestle with this is that one from 1 Corinthians 3, where Jesus is the foundation and our task is to put up the building.

First, the foundation is unique and unrepeatable. If you try to lay a foundation again you are committing apostasy. The church has so often read the Gospels as the teaching of timeless truths that it has supposed that Jesus did something for his own day and that we simply have to do the same to teach the same truths or to live the same way for our own day. Jesus, on this model, gave a great example; our task is simply to imitate him. By itself that is a radical denial of the Israel-centered plan of God and of the fact that what God did in Jesus the Messiah was unique, climactic and decisive. People who think like that sometimes end up making the cross simply the great example of self-sacrificial love instead of the moment within history when the loving God defeated the powers of evil and dealt with the sin of the world, with our sin, once and for all. That is, once more, to make the gospel good advice rather than good news. No: there is only one foundation, and whenever you are doing any building you must go back and check on that foundation to know what sort of building it already is and how you might best proceed. Before you can say "as Jesus to Israel, so the church to the world," you have to say "*because* Jesus to Israel, *therefore* the church to the world." What Jesus did was unique, climactic, decisive. That, indeed, is the ultimate theological justification for the continuing quest for the historical Jesus.

But second, once the foundation is laid, it does indeed provide the pattern, the shape, the basis, for a building to be constructed. We do not have to achieve what Jesus achieved; we cannot, and even to suppose that we might imitate him in that way would be to deny that he achieved what in fact he did. Rather—and this is absolutely crucial to understanding what is going on—our task is to *implement* his unique *achievement*. We are like the musicians called to play and sing the unique and once-only-written musical score. We don't have to write it again, but we have to play it. Or, in the image Paul uses in 1 Corinthians 3, we are now in the position of young architects discovering a wonderful foundation already laid by a master architect and having to work out what sort of a building was intended. Clearly he intended the main entrance to be here; the main rooms to be on this side, with this view; a tower at this end; and so on. When you study the Gospels, looking at the unique and unrepeatable message, challenge, warning and summons of Jesus to Israel, you are looking at the unique foundation upon which Jesus' followers must now construct the kingdom-building, the house of God, the dwelling place for God's Spirit.

In case anyone should think this is all too arbitrary, too chancy, we are promised at every turn that the Spirit of the master architect will dwell in us, nudging and guiding us, correcting mistakes, warning of danger ahead, enabling us to build—if only we will obey—with what will turn out to have been gold, silver and precious stones. "As the Father sent me, so I send you; . . . receive the Holy Spirit." These two go together. Just as in Genesis, so now in the new Genesis, the new creation, God breathes into human nostrils his own breath, and we become living stewards, looking after the garden, shaping God's world as his obedient image-bearers. Paul, indeed, uses the image of the gardener alongside that of the builder in 1 Corinthians 3. We are to implement Jesus' unique achievement.

This perspective should open the Gospels for us in a whole new way. Everything that we read there tells us something about the foundation upon which we are called to build. Everything, therefore, gives us hints about what sort of a building it is to be. As Jesus was to Israel, so the church is to be for the world.

But, you say, Israel was, *ex hypothesi,* the unique people of God, called to be the light of the world, the city on the hill that cannot be hidden. The people we minister to, the people we work with, our colleagues in the computing science laboratory or the fine arts department, the people who serve us in the grocery store or who work in the power station, are not first-century Jews. How can we summon them as Jesus summoned his contemporaries? How can we challenge them in the same way? What is the equivalent? What is the key to help us to translate Jesus' message into our own?

The key is that humans are made in the image of God. That is the equivalent, on the wider canvas, of Israel's unique position and vocation. And bearing God's image is not just a fact, it is a vocation. It means being called to reflect into the world the creative and redemptive love of God. It means being made for relationship, for stewardship, for worship—or, to put it more vividly, for sex, gardening and God. Human beings know in their bones that they are made for each other, made to look after and shape this world, made to worship the one in whose image they are made. But like Israel with her vocation, we humans get it wrong.

We worship other gods and start to reflect their likeness instead. We distort our vocation to stewardship into the will to power, treating God's world as either a gold mine or an ashtray. And we distort our calling to beautiful, healing, creative many-sided human relationships into exploitation and abuse. Marx, Nietzsche and Freud described a fallen world in which money, power and sex have become the norm, displacing relationship, stewardship and worship. Part of the point of postmodernity under the strange providence of God is to preach the Fall to arrogant modernity. What we are faced with in our culture is the post-Christian version of the doctrine of original sin: all human endeavor is radically flawed, and the journalists who take delight in pointing this out are simply telling over and over again the story of Genesis 3 as applied to today's leaders, politicians, royalty and rock stars. And our task, as image-bearing, God-loving, Christ-shaped, Spirit-filled Christians, following Christ and shaping our world, is to announce redemption to the world that has discovered its fallenness, to announce healing to the world that has discovered its brokenness, to proclaim love and trust to the world that knows only exploitation, fear and suspicion.

So the key I propose for translating Jesus' unique message to the Israel of his day into our message to our contemporaries is to grasp the parallel, which is woven deeply into both Testaments, between the human call to bear God's image and Israel's call to be the light of the world. Humans were made to reflect God's creative stewardship into the world. Israel was made to bring God's rescuing love to bear upon the world. Jesus came as the true Israel, the world's true light, and as the true image of the invisible God. He was the true Jew, the true human. He has laid the foundation, and we must build upon it. We are to be the bearers both of his redeeming love and of his creative stewardship: to celebrate it, to model it, to proclaim it, to dance to it.

"As the Father sent me, so I send you; receive the Holy Spirit; forgive sins and they are forgiven, retain them and they are retained." That last double command belongs exactly at this point. We are to go out into the world with the divine authority to forgive and retain sins. When Jesus forgave sins, they said he was blaspheming; how then can we imagine such a thing for ourselves? Answer: because of the gift of the Holy Spirit. God intends to do through us for the wider world that for which the foundation was laid in Jesus. We are to live and tell the story of the prodigal and the older brother; to announce God's glad, exuberant, richly healing welcome for sinners, and at the same time God's sorrowful but implacable opposition to those who persist in arrogance, oppression and greed. Following Christ in the power of the Spirit means bringing to our world the shape of the gospel: forgiveness, the best news that anyone can ever hear, for all who yearn for it, and judgment for all who insist on dehumanizing themselves and others by their continuing pride, injustice and greed.

See how this works out as we think very briefly through Jesus' mission to Israel, his kingdom-proclamation about which I spoke in the early chapters. Jesus announced that the moment had come, that God was at last becoming King in the way he had always intended. This was the end of exile, the defeat of evil, the return of YHWH to Zion. Very well; the first thing to say is that this happened in Jesus. God did indeed accomplish it. The foundation has been laid. The garden has been planted. The musical score is written. The principalities and powers that kept us in exile have been defeated; they need reminding of this, and we need reminding of it too, but it is a fact—if it isn't, the cross was a failure. Our task is now to build the house, to tend the garden, to play the score. The human race has been in exile; exiled from the garden, shut out of the house, bombarded with noise instead of music. Our task is to announce in deed and word that the exile is over, to enact the symbols that speak of healing and forgiveness, to act boldly in God's world in the power of the Spirit. As I suggested earlier, the proper way to expound the parables today is to ask: What should we be doing in God's world that would call forth the puzzled or even angry questions to which parables like these would be the right answer?

At the risk of trespassing in areas I know little or nothing about, let me simply hint at some ways in which this might work out. If you work in information technology, how is your discipline slanted? Is it slanted toward the will to power or the will to love? Does it exhibit the signs of technology for technology's sake, of information as a means of the oppression of those who do not have access to it by those who do? Is it developing in the service of true relationships, true stewardship and even true worship, or is it feeding and encouraging a society in which everybody creates their own private, narcissistic, enclosed world? Luther's definition of sin was *homo incurvatus in se,* "humans turned in on themselves." Does your discipline foster or challenge that? You may not be able to change the way the discipline currently works. You may be able to take some steps in that direction, given time and opportunity, but that isn't necessarily your vocation. Your task is to find the symbolic ways of doing things differently, planting flags in hostile soil, setting up signposts that say there is a different way to be human. And when people are puzzled at what you are doing, find ways—fresh ways—of telling the story of the return of the human race from its exile, and use those stories as your explanation.

Or suppose you work in fine art or music or architecture. Is your discipline still stuck in the arrogance of modernity? Or more likely, is it showing all the signs of the postmodern fragmentation, the world that declares that all great stories, all overarching systems, are power plays? Is your discipline run by people with a strong political agenda so that (say) unless you are a committed Marxist they don't think you can be a serious artist? Your calling may be to find new ways to tell the story of redemption, to create fresh symbols that will speak of a home for the homeless, the end of exile, the replanting of the garden, the rebuilding of the house. I knew a young artist who became a Christian at Oxford and struggled with tutors who despised him for it. His answer, to his own surprise, was to start painting abstract icons. They were spectacular and deeply beautiful. He didn't tell his tutors what they were until they had expressed their surprise and delight at this new turn in his work, drawing forth from him quite fresh creativity which they could not help but admire. Then when they asked what was going on, he told them the story.

So we could go on. If you are to shape your world in following Christ, it is not enough to say that being a Christian and being a professional or an academic (to address these worlds particularly for the moment) is about high moral standards, using every opportunity to talk to people about Jesus, praying for or with your students, being fair in your grading and honest in your speaking. All that is vital and necessary, but you are called to something much, much more. You are called, prayerfully, to discern where in your discipline the human project is showing signs of exile and humbly and boldly to act symbolically in ways that declare that the powers have been defeated, that the kingdom has come in Jesus the Jewish Messiah, that the new way of being human has been unveiled, and to be prepared to tell the story that explains what these symbols are all about. And in all this you are to declare, in symbol and praxis, in story and articulate answers to questions, that Jesus is Lord and Caesar is not; that Jesus is Lord and Marx, Freud and Nietzsche are not; that Jesus is Lord and neither modernity nor postmodernity is. When Paul spoke of the gospel, he was not talking primarily about a system of salvation but about the announcement, in symbol and word, that Jesus is the true Lord of the world, the true light of the world.

I am well aware that all this may seem like a counsel of perfection. Young academics want to get their Ph.D., to get a job, to get tenure, to establish themselves professionally, not least because they are aware of a vocation to teach, to write, to manage, to bring order to this part of God's world. People in other walks of life have legitimate and appropriate goals, and they need to pay their dues into the guild, to live humbly within their chosen sphere in order to attain those goals. There is a danger in Christians supposing that they simply have to be flaky, awkward, against the government all the time, continually doing things upside down and inside out. Some people of course seem to be born that way, and use the gospel imperative as an excuse for foisting their own cussedness or arrogance on everyone else. There is a need for wisdom. There is a time to speak and a time to remain silent. If it is worth working within a discipline in the first place, that is probably because there is a good deal of it that is healthy, important and to be supported. But as you pray about your work, and as in your church you and your fellow Christians are regularly planting the main symbols of the kingdom, by which I mean of course the sacraments and the inclusive family life of the people of God, you may gradually discern a sense of new things that can be done, new ways of going about your tasks. Do not despise the small but significant symbolic act. God probably does not want you to reorganize the entire discipline or the entire world of your vocation overnight. Learn to be symbol-makers and story-tellers for the kingdom of God. Learn to model true humanness in your worship, your stewardship, your relationships. The church's task vis-à-vis the world is to model genuine humanness as a sign and an invitation to those around.

As with Jesus' kingdom-announcement, this will involve retaining sins as well as forgiving them. It will involve declaring that those who persist in dehumanizing and destructive ways of going about their human tasks and goals are calling down destruction on themselves and their world. If only you had known, said Jesus, the things that make for peace! If only you had known, we must sometimes say in symbol and word, the things that make for peace, for stewardship, for justice, for love, for trust. But if you don't, your project is heading for disaster. Now, I don't recommend that a graduate student should say this to their advisory panel or tenure committee. I don't recommend it as a line to use in a job interview. There is a real danger here that Christians who have not actually done the hard work or thought through the issues will hide their incompetence behind a cheap dismissal of their academic or professional superiors as dehumanizing non-Christians. That might of course be a true assessment, but it might also be the mere sour grapes of disappointed ambition. If you have ears, then hear.

But if we are to be kingdom-announcers, modeling the new way of being human, we are also to be crossbearers. This is a strange and dark theme that is also our birthright as followers of Jesus. Shaping our world is never for a Christian a matter of going out arrogantly thinking we can just get on with the job, reorganizing the world according to some model that we have in mind. It is a matter of sharing and bearing the pain and puzzlement of the world so that the crucified love of God in Christ may be brought to bear healingly upon the world at exactly that point. Because Jesus bore the cross uniquely for us, we do not have to purchase forgiveness again; it's been done. But because, as he himself said, following him involves taking up the cross, we should expect, as the New Testament tells us repeatedly, that to build on his foundation will be to find the cross etched into the pattern of our life and work over and over again.

We would rather this were not so, and we twist and turn to avoid it. We find ourselves in Gethsemane, saying, "Lord, can this really be the way? If I have been obedient so far, why is all this happening to me? Surely you don't want me to be feeling like this?" Sometimes, indeed, the answer may be "No." It is possible that we have indeed taken a wrong road and must now turn and go by a different way. But often the answer is simply that we must stay in Gethsemane. The way of Christian witness is neither the way of quietist withdrawal, nor the way of Herodian compromise, nor the way of angry militant zeal. It is the way of being in Christ, in the Spirit, at the place where the world is in pain, so that the healing love of God may be brought to bear at that point.

This perspective is deeply rooted in New Testament theology, not least in Romans 8. There Paul speaks of the whole creation groaning together in travail. Where should the church be at such a time? Sitting smugly on the sidelines, knowing it's got the answers? No, says Paul: we ourselves groan too, because we too long for renewal, for final liberation. And where is God in all this? Sitting up in heaven wishing we could get our act together? No, says Paul (8:26-27): God is groaning too, present within the church at the place where the world is in pain. God the Spirit groans within us, calling in prayer to God the Father. The Christian vocation is to be in prayer, in the Spirit, at the place where the world is in pain, and as we embrace that vocation, we discover it to be the way of following Christ, shaped according to his messianic vocation to the cross, with arms outstretched, holding on simultaneously to the pain of the world and to the love of God.

Paul, we should note carefully, is quite clear about one thing: as we embrace this vocation, the prayer is likely to be inarticulate. It does not have to be a thought-out analysis of the problem and the solution. It is likely to be simply a groan, a groan in which the Spirit of God, the Spirit of the crucified and risen Christ, groans within us, so that the achievement of the cross might be implemented afresh at that place of pain, so that the music of the cross might be softly sung at that place of pain, so that the foundation of the cross might support a new home at that place of exile.

So if you work in government or foreign policy or finance or economics or business, you will be aware right now that the world is in pain and fear. What's happening in southeast Asia? What should we be doing in the Balkans? Is the world's financial system going to break down altogether? Are we heading for another major recession? And what can we do about the problem of major international debt? As I have argued elsewhere, I believe we are called to support the Jubilee project, which seeks to write off the huge unpayable debts of the world's poorest countries. That, I believe, would be the single best way of celebrating the millennium, and if you haven't caught up with the Jubilee movement I urge you to do so.[2] But this project can never be a way of Christians imposing a solution on the world from a great height. It will be a matter of Christians who are involved with finance and economics, with banking and business, with foreign policy and government, wrestling with the issues, often in a Gethsemane-like anguish in which the pain of the world and the healing love of God are brought together in inarticulate prayer. How much easier metaphorically to escape to Qumran and say you're just a private Christian not wanting to get involved with international finance, or to compromise with the present system and hope things will work out somehow, or to embrace a shrill and shallow agenda that has not taken seriously the depth of the problem. Some readers of this book will be called to live in that Gethsemane so that the healing love of God may reshape our world at a crucial and critical time.

Or maybe, as a student you are in a faculty or a subdiscipline that right now is facing a major split, which causes people to stop speaking to each other and to refuse to transfer each other's candidates to Ph.D. status, or to fail them when they submit their dissertations. I have known economics faculties and history faculties and others too, where half the professors are Marxists and half are not, or where half are committed postmodernists and half are not. Where should the Christian be in such a case? You may well believe that the gospel commits you to one side in the debate, though these things are rarely that easy. But my suggestion is that you see it as a call to be in prayer where your discipline is in pain. Read the Scriptures on your knees with your discipline and its problems on your heart. Come to the Eucharist and see in the breaking of the bread the broken body of Christ given for the healing of the world. Learn new ways of praying with and from the pain, the brokenness, of that crucial part of the world where God has placed you. And out of that prayer discover the ways of being peacemakers, of taking the risk of hearing both sides, of running the risk of being shot at from both sides. Are you or are you not a follower of the crucified Messiah? And of course this applies in many other areas as well: in families and marriages, in public policy and private dilemmas.

May I speak autobiographically for a moment? I have had a very clear vocation that has resulted in some very unclear choices. I live in a world that has done its best, since the Enlightenment, to separate the church from the academy. I believe passionately that this is deeply dehumanizing in both directions, and I have lived my adult life with a foot on both sides of the divide, often misunderstood by both. I live in a world where Christian devotion and evangelical piety have been highly suspicious of and sometimes implacably opposed to serious historical work on the New Testament, and vice versa. I believe passionately that this is deeply destructive of the gospel, and I have done my best to preach and to pray as a serious historian and to do my historical work as a serious preacher and pray-er. This has resulted in some fellow-historians calling me a fundamentalist and some fellow-believers calling me a compromised pseudo-liberal. The irony does not make it any less painful.

I am not looking for sympathy in saying all this. In my experience it has been precisely when I have found myself in prayer on one of those fault-lines in another private Gethsemane (and sometimes they have been moments of real agony) that I have known the presence and comfort of the living Messiah, that I have discovered that the one with whom I was wrestling and who has left me limping was none other than the angel of the Lord, and I have been reassured again and again that my calling is not necessarily to solve the great dualities of our post-Enlightenment and now postmodern world but to live in prayer at the places where the world is in pain, in the assurance that through this means, at a level far deeper than the articulate solving of the problem, my discipline may find new fruitfulness and my church, perhaps, new directions. And out of that may perhaps grow, I pray, work that is peacemaking and fruitful. The darkest times have again and again been the most productive at every level. We British don't like talking about ourselves in public, and I hesitate to hold myself up as a model, but it may be that my experience will resonate with some others who read these words and perhaps bring encouragement to some for whom Gethsemane has been hitherto an unnamed and hence misunderstood reality. "As the Father sent me," said Jesus, "so I send you; receive the Holy Spirit; forgive and retain sins." We need to reflect long upon, and to be prepared to live with, the meaning of that "as . . . so."

And of course, if we are faithful and loyal to this calling, the most frightening and unexpected thing of all, at least within many Protestant and evangelical traditions, is that we will in turn be for the world not only what Jesus was for Israel but what YHWH was and is for Israel and the world. If you believe in the presence and power of the Holy Spirit in your life, this is what it means. You are called to be truly human, but it is nothing short of the life of God within you that enables you to be so, to be remade in God's image. As C. S. Lewis said in a famous lecture, next to the sacrament itself your Christian neighbor is the holiest object ever presented to your sight, because in him or her the living Christ is truly present.[3]

We do not normally think of it like this, and we impoverish ourselves hugely as a result. We are so concerned to say at once, if anyone even suggests such an idea, that we are imperfect, weak and frail, that we fail and sin and fear and fall. And of course all that is true. But read Paul again, read John again, and discover that we are cracked vessels full of glory, wounded healers. God forgive us that we have imagined true humanness, after the Enlightenment model, to mean being successful, having it all together, knowing all the answers, never making mistakes, striding through the world as though we owned it. The living God revealed his glory in Jesus and never more clearly than when he died on the cross, crying out that he had been forsaken. When we stand in pain and prayer, following Christ and reshaping our world, we are not only discovering what it means to be truly human, we are discovering the true meaning of what the Eastern Orthodox Church refers to, yes, as "divinization." Ultimately, if you don't believe that, you don't believe in the Holy Spirit. And if you think that sounds arrogant, imagine how arrogant it would be even to think of trying to reshape our world *without* being indwelt, energized, guided and directed by God's own Spirit. Once you realize that true divinity is revealed not in self-aggrandizement, as the Enlightenment supposed, but in self-giving love, you realize that when you worship the

God revealed in Jesus and so come to reflect that God more and more the humility of God and the nobility of true humanness belong together.

In and through all of this, we are called to true *knowing*. This topic—how we know things, what knowledge is—was on the edge and sometimes at the center of many conversations that swirled around in the conference where this book had its origin. Those who are engaged in academic work are in the "knowing" business and must allow the gospel to challenge and remake their very notions of knowing. All Christians, whatever their vocation, are called to knowledge of God, of themselves, of one another, of the world. How will this work out?

We must take on board the full weight of the postmodern critique of Enlightenment theories of knowing. It is true that the much-vaunted objectivism of the Enlightenment ("we're just looking at things straight; we're just telling it like it is") was often a camouflage for political and social power and control. But when all is said and done, it is part of the essential human task given in Genesis and reaffirmed in Christ that we should *know* God, that we should know one another, that we should know God's world. Paul speaks of being "renewed in *knowledge* after the image of the creator" (Col 3:10). And this knowledge is far more than a mere guesswork that is always in danger of being deconstructed.

Current accounts of knowing have placed the would-be objective scientific knowing (test-tube epistemology, if you like) in a position of privilege. Every step away from this is seen as a step into obscurity, fuzziness and subjectivism, reaching its peaks in aesthetics and metaphysics. That is why, for instance, people have often asked me when I have spoken about Jesus in the way I have such as in this book whether I am really saying that Jesus did not "know" he was God. My answer to that is that if by "know" you mean what the Enlightenment meant, no, he did not. He had something much richer and deeper instead. We dare not, as Christians, remain content with an epistemology wished upon us from one philosophical and cultural movement, part of which was conceived in explicit opposition to Christianity. One aspect of following Jesus the Messiah is that we should allow our knowledge of him, and still more his knowledge of us, to inform us about what true knowing really is. I believe that a biblical account of "knowing" should follow the great philosopher Bernard Lonergan and take *love* as the basic mode of knowing, with the love of God as the highest and fullest sort of knowing that there is, and should work, so to speak, down from there.[4]

What is love all about? When I love, I affirm the differentness of the beloved; not to do so is of course not love at all but lust. But at the same time when I love, I am not a detached observer, the fly on the wall of objectivist epistemology. I am passionately and compassionately involved with the life and being of that—whether a thing, a person or God himself—which I am loving. In other words, though I am fully involved in the process of knowing, this does not mean that there is nothing that is being known; or to put it the other way, though I really am talking about a reality outside my own mental state, this does not mean I am a detached observer. I believe we can and must as Christians within a postmodern world give an account of human knowing that will apply to music and mathematics, to biology and history, to theology and to chemistry. We need to articulate, for the post-postmodern world, what we might call an epistemology of love.

This is at the heart of our great opportunity, here and now, for serious and joyful Christian mission to the post-postmodern world. We live at a time of cultural crisis. At the moment I don't hear anyone out there pointing a way forward out of the postmodern morass; some people are still trying to put up the shutters and live in a premodern world, many are clinging to modernism for all they're worth, and many are deciding that living off the pickings of the garbage heap of postmodernity is the best option on offer. But we can do better than that.

It isn't simply that the gospel of Jesus offers us a religious option that can outdo other religious options, that can fill more effectively the slot labeled "religion" on the cultural and social smorgasbord. The gospel of Jesus points us and indeed urges us to be at the leading edge of the whole culture, articulating in story and music and art and philosophy and education and poetry and politics and theology and even, heaven help us, biblical studies, a worldview that will mount the historically rooted Christian challenge to both modernity and postmodernity, leading the way into the post-postmodern world with joy and humor and gentleness and good judgment and true wisdom. I believe we face the question: If not now, then when? And if we are grasped by this vision, we may also hear the question: If not us, then who? And if the gospel of Jesus is not the key to this task, then what is? "As the Father sent me, so I send you; receive the Holy Spirit, forgive and retain sins."

I end with a parable and a poem. In October 1998 my wife and I went to Paris for a conference, and in a spare moment we visited the Louvre. It was the first time either of us had been there. A disappointment awaited us: the Mona Lisa, which every good tourist goes to goggle at, is not only as enigmatic as she has always been but following a violent attack is now behind thick glass. All attempts to look into those famous eyes, to face the famous questions as to what they are meaning and whether this meaning is really there or is being imposed by the viewers, are befogged by glimpses of other eyes—one's own, and dozens more besides—reflected back from the protective casing. Ah, says postmodernity, that's what all of life is like. What seems like knowledge is really the reflection of your own ideas, your own predispositions or inner world. You can't trust anything; you have to be suspicious of everything.

But is that true? I believe, and I challenge my readers to work this out in their own worlds, that there is such a thing as a love, a knowing, a hermeneutic of trust rather than suspicion, which is what we most surely need as we enter the twenty-first century:

> A Paris newcomer, I'd never been
> Followed by those dark eyes, bewitched by that
> Half-smile. Meaning, like beauty, teases, dancing
> In the soft spaces between portrait, artist,
> And the beholder's eye. But now, twice shy,
> She hides behind a veil of wood and glass;
> And we who peer and pry into her world
> See cameras, schoolchildren, other eyes,
> Other disturbing smiles. So, now, we view
> The world, each other, God, through prison glass:
> Suspicion, fear, mistrust—projections of
> Our own anxieties. Is all our knowing
> Only reflection? Let me trust, and see,
> And let love's eyes pursue, and set me free.

Notes

Chapter 1: The Challenge of Studying Jesus

[1] I have written more about this in chapter two of Marcus J. Borg and N. T. Wright, *The Meaning of Jesus: Two Visions* (San Francisco: HarperSanFrancisco; London: SPCK, 1999).

[2] On the whole quest, see now the fascinating and wide-ranging account by Charlotte Allen, *The Human Christ: The Search for the Historical Jesus* (New York: Free Press; Oxford: Lion, 1998).

[3] I have in mind, among other writers, John Dominic Crossan, *The Historical Jesus: The Life of a Mediterranean Jewish Peasant* (San Francisco: HarperSanFrancisco; Edinburgh: T & T Clark, 1991).

[4] For a full critique of the Jesus Seminar's flagship product, *The Five Gospels*, ed. Robert W. Funk and Roy W. Hoover (New York: Macmillan, 1993); see N. T. Wright, "Five Gospels but No Gospel: Jesus and the Seminar," in *Authenticating the Activities of Jesus*, ed. Bruce Chilton and Craig A. Evans (Leiden: Brill, 1999), pp. 83-120.

[5] See N. T. Wright, *Jesus and the Victory of God* (Minneapolis: Augsburg Fortress, 1996), pp. 246-58; and chapter two of this work.

[6] I here summarize very briefly the material set out in *Jesus and the Victory of God*, chaps. 1-3, and in my article "Historical Jesus (Quest for)" in *Anchor Bible Dictionary*, ed. D. N. Freedman, 6 vols. (New York: Doubleday, 1992), 3:796-802.

[7] See Luke Timothy Johnson, *The Real Jesus* (San Francisco: HarperSanFrancisco, 1995).

[8] Ben Meyer, *The Aims of Jesus* (Philadelphia: Fortress; London: SCM Press, 1979).

[9] E. P. Sanders, *Jesus and Judaism* (Philadelphia: Fortress; London: SCM Press, 1985).

[10] See James M. Robinson, *A New Quest of the Historical Jesus* (London: SCM Press, 1959).

[11] See Robert W. Funk, *Honest to Jesus: Jesus for a New Millennium* (San Francisco: HarperSanFrancisco, 1996).

[12] Cf. N. T. Wright, *The New Testament and the People of God* (Minneapolis: Augsburg Fortress, 1992), pt. 2.

Chapter 2: The Challenge of the Kingdom

[1] The clearest example of this belief is Daniel 9:2, 24, where it is stated that instead of the exile lasting for seventy years, as Jeremiah had prophesied, it would actually last for "seventy weeks of years," that is, 490 years. The same belief, in the continuation of a theological state of affairs that can fairly be described through the metaphor of "ongoing exile," is witnessed in literally dozens of places in second-temple Judaism. See now the essay by Craig A. Evans "Jesus and the Continuing Exile of Israel," in *Jesus & the Restoration of Israel: A Critical Assessment of N. T. Wright's "Jesus and the Victory of God,"* ed. Carey C. Newman (Downers Grove, Ill.: InterVarsity Press, 1999), pp. 67-90; and cf. N. T. Wright, *The New Testament and the People of God* (Minneapolis: Augsburg Fortress, 1992), pp. 268-72; N. T. Wright, *Jesus and the Victory of God*

(Minneapolis: Augsburg Fortress, 1996), pp. xvii-xviii, 126-29 and frequently elsewhere.

[2]Is 13:10.

[3]On this whole topic see especially chapter ten of Wright, *New Testament*; and at a more popular level chapter two of N. T. Wright, *The Millennium Myth* (Louisville, Ky.: Westminster John Knox; London: SPCK, 1999).

[4]On the Pharisees see especially Wright, *New Testament*, pp. 181-203.

[5]See Wright, *Jesus and the Victory of God*, pp. 230-39.

[6]Is 40:8; 55:10-11,13.

[7]Is 6:9-13; cf. Is 10:33—11:1.

[8]Cf. Jn 12:40; Acts 28:26-27.

[9]See Wright, *Jesus and the Victory of God*, pp. 125-31.

[10]Josephus *Life* 110.

[11]Mk 1:44.

[12]See Mt 10:6, 23; 15:24, alongside 8:11-12. This perspective seems to have been acknowledged and respewed in the early church; see, e.g., Rom 15:8-9.

Chapter 3: The Challenge of the Symbols

[1]For the details of this and the subsequent arguments, see N. T. Wright, *Jesus and the Victory of God* (Minneapolis: Augsburg Fortress, 1996), chap. 9. Sanders's views are expounded in E. P. Sanders, *Jesus and Judaism* (Philadelphia: Fortress; London: SCM Press, 1985); and *The Historical Figure of Jesus* (London: Penguin, 1993).

[2]Philo *Special Laws* 2.253.

[3]Wright, *Jesus and the Victory of God*, p. 392.

[4]Lk 13:10-17; 14:1-6.

[5]Mt 8:21-22 par. Lk 9:59-60; Mt 10:34-39; Mk 3:33 par. Mt 12:48.

[6]Mishnah *Aboth* 3.2.

[7]Josephus *Antiquities* 14.415f.; 15.345-48.

[8]Cf. N. T. Wright, *The New Testament and the People of God* (Minneapolis: Augsburg Fortress, 1992), p. 234f.

[9]Cf. Wright, *Jesus and the Victory of God*, pp. 439-42.

[10]Cf. ibid., pp. 467-72.

Chapter 4: The Crucified Messiah

[1]This argument corresponds in outline to N. T. Wright, *Jesus and the Victory of God* (Minneapolis: Augsburg Fortress, 1996), chap. 11.

[2]This argument summarizes Wright, *Jesus and the Victory of God*, chap. 12.

[3]Michael O. Wise, *The First Messiah: Investigating the Savior Before Christ* (San Francisco: HarperSanFrancisco, 1999). The fact that this book overstates its case somewhat should not blind us to the obvious point: that it is perfectly possible to study the motivation of a figure within a particular culture and furthermore that there are models within second-temple Judaism of how leaders constructed that motivation, that sense of vocation, not least out of the scriptural narratives as they were being reread at the time.

[4]For the details, cf. Wright, *Jesus and the Victory of God*, pp. 513-19.

[5]11Q13 identifies the one who announces the Isaianic good news as himself the Messiah; 4Q521 frag. 2 attributes the healings of Isaiah 35 to the Messiah, a theme that finds an echo in Matthew 11:2-15. The Qumran texts may now be found in one of the readily available English translations, e.g., Geza Vermes, *The Dead Sea Scrolls in*

English, 5th ed. (Harmondsworth, England: Penguin, 1997).

[6]Jacob Neusner, "Money-Changers in the Temple: The Mishnah's Explanation," *New Testament Studies* 35 (1989): 287-90.

[7]Wright, *Jesus and the Victory of God,* p. 564f.

[8]Mt 23:37-38; Lk 13:34-35.

[9]Mk 10:38-40.

[10]Mk 8:31; 9:12, 31; 10:32-34, 45; and the parallels in Matthew and Luke.

[11]For the details in each case see Wright, *Jesus and the Victory of God,* pp. 579-84.

[12]Ibid., p. 591.

[13]Ibid., p. 596.

[14]Ibid., pp. 609-10.

Chapter 5: Jesus & God

[1]The original lecture on which this chapter was based also contributed material to chapter ten of Marcus J. Borg and N. T. Wright, *The Meaning of Jesus: Two Visions* (San Francisco: HarperSanFrancisco; London: SPCK, 1999).

[2]For full details, see N. T. Wright, *Jesus and the Victory of God* (Minneapolis: Augsburg Fortress, 1996), pp. 615-29.

[3]See N. T. Wright, *The Climax of the Covenant: Christ and the Law in Pauline Theolog* (Minneapolis: Fortress; Edinburgh: T & T Clark, 1991), chaps. 4, 5, 6; N. T. Wright *What St. Paul Really Said* (Grand Rapids, Mich.: Eerdmans; Oxford: Lion, 1997), chap 4. Colossians is sometimes considered post-Pauline, but the passage in question is sometimes considered to be an earlier poem incorporated into the letter.

[4]See e.g., Richard J. Bauckham, "The Worship of Jesus in Apocalyptic Christianity," *New Testament Studies* 27 (1981): 322-41.

[5]For an earlier discussion of the first two false trails, see pages 74-75.

[6]2 Sam 7:1-3.

[7]2 Sam 7:11-14. The promise is repeated in, e.g., Ps 2:7; 89:26-27. Second Samuel 7 and Psalm 2 are combined, along with other texts, in 4Q174, a Qumran anthology of messianic proof-texts.

[8]Mt 8:4; Mk 1:44; Lk 5:14.

[9]See Jacob Neusner, *A Rabbi Talks with Jesus: An Intermillennial, Interfaith Exchange* (New York: Doubleday, 1993).

[10]Mishnah *Aboth* 3.2; cf. the discussion in 3.8.

[11]Mk 4:14.

[12]Cf., Ps 33:6; Is 40:8; 55:11.

[13]Mt 8:8; 8:16.

[14]Mt 12:28. The parallel in Luke (11:20) has "finger" rather than "spirit."

[15]E.g., Mt 25:1-13; cf. Wright, *Jesus and the Victory of God,* pp. 311-16; Ben Witherington III, *Jesus the Sage: The Pilgrimage of Wisdom* (Minneapolis: Fortress, 1994).

[16]Cf. Wright, *Jesus and the Victory of God,* pp. 612-15, 631-42.

[17]On this whole topic see chapter fourteen of Borg and Wright, *The Meaning of Jesus.*

[18]For more details, cf. Wright, *Jesus and the Victory of God,* pp. 632-37.

[19]Mk 12:35, with parallels in Matthew and Luke.

[20]For more details, cf. Wright, *Jesus and the Victory of God,* pp. 642-45.

[21]Ibid., p. 651.

[22]Ibid., p. 653.

[23]This paragraph is slightly adapted from Wright, *Jesus and the Victory of God,* p. 653.

[24]From here to the end of the chapter I am borrowing, and adapting, material from my lecture published as "A Biblical Portrait of God," in N. T. Wright, Keith Ward and Brian Hebblethwaite, *The Changing Face of God: Lincoln Lectures in Theology 1996* (Lincoln: Lincoln Studies in Theology 2), pp. 9-29.

Chapter 6: The Challenge of Easter

[1]John Dominic Crossan, *The Historical Jesus: The Life of a Mediterranean Jewish Peasant* (San Francisco: HarperSanFrancisco; Edinburgh: T & T Clark, 1991), p. xxvii.

[2]Barbara Thiering, *Jesus the Man* (New York: Bantam, 1994). Her most recent venture in the same genre, *The Book That Jesus Wrote* (New York: Bantam, 1998), proposes that Jesus himself was the author of John's Gospel.

[3]G. Vermes, *Jesus the Jew: A Historian's Reading of the Gospels* (London: Collins, 1973), pp. 37-41.

[4]E. P. Sanders, *Jesus and Judaism* (Philadelphia: Fortress; London: SCM Press, 1985), pp. 320, 340.

[5]I have spelled this argument out more fully in two articles in the *Sewanee Theological Review* 41, no. 2 (1998): 107-40.

[6]For more detail, cf. N. T. Wright, *The New Testament and the People of God* (Minneapolis: Augsburg Fortress, 1992), pp. 320-34.

[7]Mt 27:51-54.

[8]John Dominic Crossan, *Jesus: A Revolutionary Biography* (San Francisco: HarperSan-Francisco, 1994), chap. 6.

[9]See Wright, *New Testament*, pp. 241-43.

[10]This is the significance of Paul's quotation, in 15:27, of Psalm 8:6 ("God has put all things in subjection under his feet").

[11]Cf. 1 Cor 9:1.

[12]Cf. Acts 12:15; 23:8-10.

Chapter 7: Walking to Emmaus in a Postmodern World

[1]I here need to repeat a little of what I said in *The Millennium Myth* (Louisville, Ky.: Westminster John Knox; London: SPCK, 1999), chap. 3.

[2]See N. T. Wright, *What St. Paul Really Said* (Grand Rapids, Mich.: Eerdmans; Oxford: Lion, 1997), chap. 7.

[3]E. E. Ellis, *The Gospel of Luke* (Nashville and London: Nelson, 1966), ad loc.

Chapter 8: The Light of the World

[1]See N. T. Wright, *New Heavens, New Earth: The Biblical Picture of Christian Hope*, Grove Biblical Series 11 (Cambridge: Grove, 1999).

[2]See especially chapter five of N. T. Wright, *The Millennium Myth* (Louisville, Ky.: Westminster John Knox; London: SPCK, 1999).

[3]C. S. Lewis, "The Weight of Glory," in *Screwtape Proposes a Toast and Other Pieces*.

[4]On Lonergan see the writings of Ben F. Meyer, particularly *The Aims of Jesus* (Philadelphia: Fortress, 1978); and *Critical Realism and the New Testament* (Allison Park, Penn.: Pickwick, 1989).

Index